Helping Students
with Study Problems

SRHE and Open University Press Imprint
General Editor: Heather Eggins

Current titles include:

Ronald Barnett: *The Idea of Higher Education*
Ronald Barnett: *Improving Higher Education*
Ronald Barnett: *Learning to Effect*
Ronald Barnett: *Limits of Competence*
Tony Becher: *Governments and Professional Education*
Robert Bell and Malcolm Tight: *Open Universities: A British Tradition?*
Hazel Bines and David Watson: *Developing Professional Education*
Jean Bocock and David Watson: *Managing the Curriculum*
David Boud *et al.*: *Using Experience for Learning*
John Earwaker: *Helping and Supporting Students*
Roger Ellis: *Quality Assurance for University Teaching*
Gavin J. Fairbairn and Christopher Winch: *Reading, Writing and Reasoning: A Guide for Students*
Shirley Fisher: *Stress in Academic Life*
Diana Green: *What is Quality in Higher Education?*
Jill Johnes and Jim Taylor: *Performance Indicators in Higher Education*
Ian McNay: *Visions of Post-compulsory Education*
Robin Middlehurst: *Leading Academics*
Henry Miller: *Managing Change in Universities*
Jennifer Nias: *The Human Nature of Learning: Selections from the Work of M.L.J. Abercrombie*
Keith Allan Noble: *Changing Doctoral Degrees*
Gillian Pascall and Roger Cox: *Women Returning to Higher Education*
Graham Peeke: *Mission and Change*
Moira Peelo: *Helping Students with Study Problems*
Kjell Raaheim *et al.*: *Helping Students to Learn*
Tom Schuller: *The Future of Higher Education*
Michael Shattock: *The UGC and the Management of British Universities*
Geoffrey Squires: *First Degree*
Ted Tapper and Brian Salter: *Oxford, Cambridge and the Changing Idea of the University*
Kim Thomas: *Gender and Subject in Higher Education*
Malcolm Tight: *Higher Education: A Part-time Perspective*
David Warner and Gordon Kelly: *Managing Educational Property*
David Warner and Charles Leonard: *The Income Generation Handbook*
Sue Wheeler and Jan Birtle: *A Handbook for Personal Tutors*
Thomas G. Whiston and Roger L. Geiger: *Research and Higher Education*
Gareth Williams: *Changing Patterns of Finance in Higher Education*
John Wyatt: *Commitment to Higher Education*

Helping Students with Study Problems

Moira Peelo

The Society for Research into Higher Education
& Open University Press

Published by SRHE and
Open University Press
Celtic Court
22 Ballmoor
Buckingham
MK18 1XW

and
1900 Frost Road, Suite 101
Bristol, PA 19007, USA

First Published 1994

A catalogue record of this book is available from the British Library

ISBN 0 335 19307 2 (pb)   0 335 19308 0 (hb)

A Library of Congress Cataloging-in-Publication number is available for this title

Typeset by Graphicraft Typesetters Ltd, Hong Kong
Printed in Great Britain by St Edmundsbury Press Ltd,
Bury St Edmunds, Suffolk

Contents

Acknowledgements

I would like to acknowledge my counselling colleagues over the years: Rachel Rogers and Shirley Brown, who started me in this direction; Sandra Burr; Isobel Derricourt; Trish di Cesare; John Elder; Pam Gilbert; Michael Hammond; Kate Hewer; Paul Pavli; Sue Smith; Maureen Sheron, who kindly read earlier drafts of some chapters; and my colleagues on the Effective Learning Programme, Gordon Clark, Janet Clements and Rosemary Turner. Brian Francis and Keith Soothill provided support and encouragement. I would also like to thank the many students I have worked with, and hope that they have gained as much as I have through our meetings.

1

Introduction

This book arises out of my experience of helping students with study problems. This is not precisely the same as 'study skills' teaching, as it is commonly called. Instead, I am talking about ways of helping students after everything they know about study has let them down. I meet many students in one-to-one interviews, during which we co-operate to find novel and individual ways out of personal work crises. This book describes that practice, along with ideas for preventive teaching through workshops – that is, the more traditional 'study skills' teaching sessions for people who have not run into study crises. The underlying philosophy in both cases is a belief that study has an emotional impact on people's lives as well as an intellectual one, and that academic development is an integral part of personal development. Rather than assuming that learning happens to individuals in vacuums, the assumption is made that academic and personal development takes place in specific social settings, which influence the processes and experience of learning.

I use the word 'counselling' in a loose way, as a shorthand to describe meetings with individual students in need of help with study, as opposed to running groups or workshops or teaching study techniques (although all of these form a part of my activities at different times). I do believe that it is the relationship between study counsellor and individual student which brings about change. It is a relationship which should be built on trust, safety, confidentiality, mutual respect and absence of judgemental attitudes. However, this book does not add to the wider debate about whether counselling is a relationship, a philosophy or a technique, and I will not be taking part in a discussion about the true nature of counselling, or whether specialist counsellors are possible or desirable. In addition to the expression 'study counsellor', I also use the phrases 'study tutor', 'tutor/counsellor', or sometimes just 'tutor', to embrace the range of situations in which staff are approached by individual students with study problems. The word 'counsellor' is used to denote a relationship which is quite different to the traditional teacher–student one. The role of study counsellor teeters on the edge between academic support and welfare support, which can be quite separate structures in different institutions. This structural divide between academic and pastoral concerns can set up tension when both elements meet in individuals carrying out particular roles – such as personal counsellors or seminar tutors – and stirs up confusion about what is appropriate behaviour in these roles. Whoever 'owns' the job of providing study support, I am referring to the activity of helping students who face problems with study, either by their own or others' definitions. Study counselling, whoever carries it out, is about helping people to locate, recognize and use their own and external resources in the face of academic challenges.

For me, individual meetings about study problems have always taken place in a student counselling service, away from the pressures of appraisal and assessment inherent in teaching relationships. The word 'counselling' is used here to summarize an approach which is not dependent on the amount of time available to spend with individual students or on the specific techniques used. Rather, the approach is based on an attitude of mind which is: to start from where the student is rather than imposing a specific style of study or a pre-established set of solutions. That approach also implies, for me, an ethical code or set of preferred practices. The most important element of these is confidentiality.

1. Students must know that they can relax and have complete confidence that only with their permission will anything discussed be relayed to others outside the counselling service. This extends to ensuring that any letters written about students or on behalf of students are read by them before being posted.
2. Closely connected with confidentiality is the desire to use students for research purposes. There is no problem if this is made plain from the beginning, but there are profound ethical issues surrounding offers of help which are research in disguise.
3. Study counsellors should take care, if *current* written assignments are being used as a basis for working on study problems, that students are always clear and confident that it is their own work which goes to tutors for marking. Special dispensations might have to be negotiated and agreed in individual cases, such as with non-native students with language problems or people with severe specific learning difficulties.
4. The role is one which should support students in increasing confidence in their academic work, helping students to find their own ways of working and fulfilling personal ambitions, rather than imposing 'correct' ways of studying. While techniques of study can be usefully learnt, care should be taken not to give the impression that there are a set of agreed techniques which just need to be applied regardless of circumstances or course content.
5. Suggesting techniques to try out is different than laying down the law about what study should be. Building confidence is more than just developing personal approaches to study, it is about having a clear sense

of academic identity. So study counselling means knowing where a student starts and the counsellor ends – and not compromising the student's autonomy.

6. Study counselling practices will always reflect an underlying view of the concept of intelligence – and, hence, whether or not a counsellor thinks adults are capable of improving their academic performance. Study counsellors should sort out their thinking on this before offering to support people who are struggling to improve their work.

I use the word 'student' to refer to anyone attending a full- or part-time undergraduate course. These days, students come in a wider range of shapes, sizes and ages than has been the case in the past. Some may only spend part of the week as a student, and the rest of their lives can be taken up with important responsibilities and decisions, through family life or paid employment. Although most are white, recent school-leavers, this is no longer exclusively the case. The degree-level courses these students attend are available in a range of colleges of higher and further education as well as in universities old, new, civic or redbrick – for the word 'university' covers a range of institutions. I use the word 'university' in this book only because I have carried out my study work in one.

Throughout the book are exercises to be used by academic staff, students, trainee counsellors and any other interested groups, either to think about alone or to adapt for group work. As well as suggestions for one-to-one work, some exercises are designed specifically with workshops in mind. All workshop teaching requires a leap of imagination, and trainers are always in the business of taking, borrowing and adapting new ideas to suit their circumstances. These exercises are intended to be used in that way, rather than meant as recipes to be followed to the letter.

From time to time I list my hopes for students, for example what I see as progress for students with reading-related problems. I do this because it is often assumed that to be non-judgemental is to lack opinions and thoughts of one's own – which is, of course, rubbish. What matters is that you know your own views and have a clear sense of where you end and the student begins – in other words that you do not let your opinion get in the way of someone else's development.

The next chapter lays out my experience and philosophy of study counselling, what the job might reasonably be expected to involve, and some issues concerning the context in which it takes place. Chapter 3 describes how to get started in helping students to define and describe their problems, while usually under the twin pressures of deadlines and backlogs of work. In Chapter 4 the aim of helping a student to improve in academic work while taking account of the emotional underpinnings of work crises and study is explored further, particularly concentrating on what this means in practice for a tutor/counsellor.

Reading and writing are two sides of the same coin, so the separation made here is arbitrary but made in order to discuss the relevant issues.

Chapter 5 considers ways of approaching reading when students have become 'stuck' with their work, usually by falling behind with written assignments, and Chapter 6 explores ways of tackling 'being stuck' which are closely linked to writing. Chapter 7 moves on from getting restarted with reading and writing, and looks in a little more depth at the ways in which self and the ability to communicate are interlinked.

Anxiety and fear can permeate all aspects of study, and Chapter 8 looks at two triggers which cause particular distress – fear in relation to examinations and mathematical work. Chapter 9 examines how the general philosophy described throughout the book is carried into 'preventive' work when running workshops for students. In the final chapter I look at the implications of this approach to study problems for degree-level teaching and finish by asking the question: whose degree is it?

Throughout the book I use imaginary conversations to give a flavour of common conversational styles. This is deliberately chosen as a technique to elaborate my own practice without using 'case material'. While the conversations are fictitious, they are all discussions which could happen in any meeting between student and study counsellor.

2

Background, Assumptions and Myths

My experience of study counselling

After eight years of working with individual students who are facing problems with their academic work I have developed certain beliefs. While the academic ideal may be to produce work which is dispassionate in style, we confuse this 'detached' end-product with the process of learning. The process of learning is emotional, it can be fun, dreary, elating, disheartening, adventurous, terrifying and any other emotion experienced by people formally enrolled on courses of study. We mistakenly approach intellectual activity as if it were any other bodily function which has a physical life of its own separate from the rest of our existences. So your cat has died, your girlfriend has left you and you have nowhere to live, and yet you are surprised that you seem unable to write essays. There is an expectation that when study has gone wrong, there are techniques available which can be applied quite regardless of individuals and their lives, rather like taking indigestion tablets. In addition, I assume that students' prior experiences and interactions within the social setting of universities and colleges have important effects upon the experience of undergraduate learning.

In 1985 I agreed to offer support to my local university's student counselling service in the area of 'study skills', as it was then generally called. At that point it was not clear whether my views and those of counsellors would be sufficiently compatible to allow this to be a useful arrangement, so we were all happy to move slowly. I started by seeing a very few people who had been referred to me by other counsellors. It was also hoped that I might offer a link between the counselling service and relevant research into student learning, and offer 'back-up' to counsellors who might wish to discuss study issues arising from their work but without always referring students directly to me. Most students that I meet come to me as a last resort when their capacity to work appears to have broken down and their usual patterns of working are no longer sufficient for the tasks they must complete. Sometimes this is part of or precipitates a personal crisis which can be quite wide-reaching. Many have been through pre-university study courses, during-university study sessions, and have read or own a large pile of study skills manuals, and people feel quite ashamed that they seem unable to unravel study difficulties by themselves. This can trigger a confirmation of their own stupidity – 'I always knew I was not good enough, and this just proves it.'

I work alongside people with study problems, doing whatever seems necessary to help them get whatever it is they want out of their studies. I do not offer tutoring in individual subjects. I do not offer help with depression, schizophrenia, phobias, anxiety, addictions, relationships, eating problems, bereavement or any of the other problems which people experience. However, any of these (not yet all at one and the same time) may be central issues, important issues, relevant issues in students' lives, so I need to be aware of what these problems might imply. I do not offer a curative or therapeutic relationship. I am prepared to act as 'sticking plaster' and work alongside students who wish to complete work, without tackling major personal issues, if that is what they wish and if it is possible.

It is difficult to summarize all the years of working with individual students facing study problems. Sometimes it is appropriate to talk in technical terms, acting as a guide, interpreting the institution's demands. Sometimes it is listening while frustration, disappointments, daydreams, ambitions, hopes are disentangled. It is acting as a 'sounding board' for a specific piece of writing. It is being a teacher, instructing on what essay-writing, reading, note-taking can be. It can be about challenging inflexible ideas about what learning is. Sometimes it is waiting until a student summons enough confidence to write their view without feeling terrorized.

The work can include writing notes, making telephone calls and writing letters to departments on behalf of students, on occasion making telephone calls to students temporarily away from the university, meeting members of families, meeting members of staff, advising on study teaching, designing, preparing and running workshops, making referrals where appropriate and advising on study-related issues within and without the counselling service. I have learnt that 'study' is also an emotive issue for those referring students, and referrals often tell as much about staff members' views of what study is about as they do about the student concerned. The variety of views can be stimulating if you work with humorous and insightful colleagues, but hell if there is not proper support and care for study counsellors, their needs and their role.

Over the years since 1985 the number of referrals has increased considerably, but we have tried to maintain a principle of flexibility by responding to the 'surges' in demand which happen at different times during the academic year. Traditionally the first weeks of the autumn term have seen fewer one-to-one meetings; instead I tend to work with students already known to me from the preceding year. Students are usually trying to finish work which has been allowed an extension over the summer vacation. The last weeks before the Easter vacation have invariably seen a rush of students whose study problems have been around for some time, but who thought they could get by. Students may have large backlogs of work from before Christmas as well as from the current term. However, these traditional patterns have begun to shift and change in recent years, as universities have become more adventurous in ways of assessing students and in the kinds of tasks set and as the numbers of students have increased.

During the 1980s less attention was paid to individual study problems, but 'how to do a degree' has come back into fashion, so students have a wider set of choices about how to get help. In the early days, however, doing study work inevitably meant putting on workshops about all aspects of completing degrees. There are two approaches to 'preventive' teaching: one is to combine study work with course content in academic departments. This has the advantage of not objectifying study or reducing it to a set of techniques to be applied in any circumstances. The other is to provide 'open' workshops for all interested students, which treats study as separate from departmental matters. This has the advantage of allowing students to experiment with new ideas anonymously and away from the situation in which they are assessed. As interest in study grows, open workshops allow the possibility of students having access to the ideas of quite different presenters.

For some years I have been involved with a team which arranges open study sessions and workshops for undergraduates. My aims for the course were different to my intentions in one-to-one study work: to foster the view that it is normal to examine and develop study habits; to allow students the chance to think about study practices without the pressures of assessment; to provide a course which covers the basics about university study; and to enable students to be taught by specialists they are unlikely otherwise to meet. We started by inviting suggestions for the content of the proposed programme from all members of the university, and asking them to contribute if they should so wish. The response to this enabled us to incorporate new ideas with those already developed via our own experience of workshops and those put forward by students. Schemes often falter because they are dependent on one person. It was our intention to plan a course in such a way as to make it possible for the programme to be maintained, and to a professional standard, when the time came for the original administrators to move on.

The programme for the year includes sessions on: academic writing; reading; report-writing for scientists; memory; time management; project planning; presentation skills; revision; sitting examinations; and relaxation. We wanted presenters to be people who met another aim – which is to have thought about either student learning or their own specialization in depth – and are innovators in what they do.

One-to-one study work: underlying philosophy

The philosophy which underlies my work with individual students is best understood as shaped by the person-centred tradition of counselling, of which Carl Rogers is the most famous exponent. My interest in counselling theory started in the mid-1970s when employed to carry out research into tertiary education by interviewing students. At that time interviewing was not commonly used in research and there was no formal help available, so as part of my trial-and-error introduction to research I enrolled for evening classes in anything which seemed remotely relevant. What attracted me then, and now, about Rogerian counselling was the respect shown to clients, and the assumption that they retained control and ownership of their lives and problems. While I have arguments with practising Rogerian counsellors and with aspects of Rogers's writing, I still believe that the process by which clients find their own solutions is as important as the solutions found; and that, initially, Rogers provided a vocabulary by which people like me could dispense with 'expert' knowledge and diagnoses where these were inappropriately or invasively employed. While some might find it hard to see how academic work fits into this person-centred tradition, my views can be roughly summarized as: a belief that an empathic listener can introduce people to their intellectual selves, which are as much an integral part of humans as their physical or emotional beings. Intellectual development is not a physical process like digestion, rather it is about choices, preferences and ways of living, while communicating these elements of being within a specific academic medium and setting. As with all life, then, intellectual development is expressed in an unceasing conversation between an individual and particular parts of a social world.

The impact of real listening is impossible to quantify, but most of us experience once in a lifetime the powerful force of being heard. Mearns and Thorne (1988: 104) well describe the solace of being truly heard when going through crisis: 'The experience of being deeply understood and the sense of companionship which springs from this are in themselves powerful antidotes to the overwhelming feelings of powerlessness which can be the concomitants of crisis.' 'Empathy' has come to mean the capacity to use one's imagination to understand what it feels like to be *that* person in *that* situation, without losing hold of one's own sense of self. It has not always had such positive connotations: psychotherapy and counselling have always been concerned with theory and research, and Sullivan used 'empathy' to refer to the process of transmission of anxiety from mother to child. Mabel Cohen, in the introduction to the 1953 compilation of Sullivan's work, says that the term was used not to denote some form of extra-sensory perception but to indicate that the process was not understood because it had not been investigated (Sullivan 1953: xvi). Rogers (1967: 331–2) presented empathic understanding as a part solution to the barrier to communication set up by constant evaluation: listening with understanding, which 'means to see the expressed idea and attitude from the other person's point of view, to sense how it feels to him, to achieve his frame of reference in regard to the thing he is talking about'. Not allowing the same conditions to study counselling as to any other sort of counselling springs from a twofold lack of thought: first, doubting the clients' panic and emotions, and judging that because they are only triggered by study, they are not 'real' emotions; and second, using our personal estimation of the role of study in our own lives as a basis for judging what role it should play in students' lives, regardless of the students' clear message that academic work might play a quite distinct or different role in their lives.

For those of us brought up to see study as being about the mechanistic application of technical rules which, somehow, come naturally to those with sufficient innate ability, Carl Rogers's *Freedom to Learn* and subsequent revision, *Freedom to Learn for the 80s*, had to come as a breath of fresh air. For example, Rogers (1983: 259) described in human terms how technique and ability are not sufficient in coming to terms with 'study' problems:

> A boy senses, though perhaps not consciously, that he is more loved and prized by his parents when he thinks of being a doctor than when he thinks of being an artist. Gradually he introjects the values attached to being a doctor. He comes to want, above all, to be a doctor. Then in college he is baffled by the fact that he repeatedly fails in chemistry, which is absolutely necessary to becoming a physician, in spite of the fact that the guidance counselor assures him he has the ability to pass the course. Only in counseling interviews does he begin to realize how completely he has lost touch with his organismic reactions, how out of touch he is with his own valuing process.

As a social scientist, the attraction of Egan's (1975) later development of person-centred work to accommodate an awareness of the impact, often damaging, of the social world on individuals had to be attractive to me. At its worst, superficial interpretations of Rogerian work can seem like a 'nodding dog' school of care; if coupled with an assumption that all human beings have entirely free choices, if they but realized it, the resultant level of naivety can allow no room for issues of power and harm. Individuals have limited power in social settings: education, in Britain, has given access to qualifications, which in turn have given access to interesting, well-paid jobs. The economic, political and social power associated, in our society, with some levels of paid employment is not, therefore, available to most who do not reach certain standards in formal education. Qualifications have never been enough of themselves to gain access to valued prizes, but credentials ensure that the gate swings slightly open. It follows, then, that we do not encourage in education those we do not perceive as appropriate holders of prized occupations (Peelo 1988), hence education touches on far more than study techniques alone – it encompasses all that we feel about ourselves and our places (right or wrong) in the wider world. My interest, ultimately, lies not in therapeutic relationships, however valuable they are, but in opening access to education, so that by learning to study more freely, potential is developed and *real* choices become possible, along with the satisfactions of intellectual curiosity and pursuits. Among the tools of the comfortable student (whether officially enrolled on recognized courses or not) are those which help them translate the codes of closed groups into manageable and comprehensible units.

The old expression 'non-directive' has always evoked anxiety in caring people, as it can stir up a sense of helplessness in many when faced with human suffering but told that they cannot 'do' anything to transform people's lives and that advice is of little use. The question asked is: 'What else is there that I can do?' With study this question is especially heartfelt, as there is the strong temptation to lapse into expert 'teacher' mode and talk *at* unhappy students. Being 'non-directive' in one-to-one study work is not just a matter of preference, but also a pragmatic awareness that if the students have already exhausted most other routes, giving direct advice is merely repeating what has not worked previously. The more productive line of work is to explore why particular approaches have not already worked for an individual. While the approach is 'person-centred' in origins, one-to-one study work needs you to give of yourself as a fellow-learner. Rather than being an expert who 'owns' study, you need to be able to be present as a fellow-traveller. This means offering materials and ideas for students to try out and explore without deploying didactic teaching habits and without attachment to pet techniques regardless of students' responses. Mearns and Thorne (1988: 2) have described the need for person-centred counsellors to offer complete concentration and awareness of their own feelings, responses and intuitions as well as those of the client, and this is no less so for study, where one's responses to clients and one's relationship with learning are present as influential elements in the relationship. These responses are coupled with the desire to enable students to have time and safe opportunity to explore their attitudes to study, its meaning in their lives and its pains. The practice of working with students with study problems, however, does not take place in isolation from the rest of the world, but is influenced by wider, popular views of education.

The assumption, for example, that all students are privileged and have never faced problems at school or in life is commonplace. This is rarely so for late returners to degree work, and cannot be assumed about younger undergraduates either. My first meetings with students are usually shaped by expectations of a mechanistic approach to study in spite of the distress work problems may have caused. And it can seem that all other students know the answers about how to study, and have cracked the secret codes. Students are supposed to be bright, and so they assume that they should be able to solve problems: academic problems, in particular, should be within their domain, so there is a double burden of worry. As well as not being able to work, students fear that there must be something wrong with them, that they must be less able than other students by definition, or they would not have problems.

The structure of degree courses is not encouraging, for few institutions run the supervision sessions popularly associated with universities, in which a tutor meets one or two students only. Instead, the smallest groups have at least six or more undergraduates in them (and this would be a luxury in most institutions), so those who do not know what is expected of them on arrival feel at a disadvantage and have few of the sorts of meeting with staff in which they can test out what seems to be expected. Written assignments then become the main means of finding out what is required of the student, but as these are produced in order to be assessed few new students can be sufficiently relaxed to use their writing to explore institutional expectations. Late returners to formal education often believe that they are stupid and, indeed, may have built their pre-degree lives round a specific, non-academic, image of themselves. It is hard to change round one's self-image, and students of all ages build up elaborate structures, often unawares, to hide from the world what they perceive as the depth of their stupidity. Writing, then, is fraught with dangers as it is an ideal opportunity to be exposed as a fraud, and if final marks have a heavy weighting to coursework assessment, the amount of writing in the time available can make these underlying doubts and fears unbearable. The pressure to avoid being found out triggers blocks of many varieties, and obliges students to work to unrealistically high standards. And returning to formal education can stir up a mass of dimly remembered anxieties formed by adult cruelty in earlier schooling.

Techniques of study have their place in study counselling, but cannot be an end in themselves. Making clear that there is no one right way of studying and that it is a process of trial and error is a necessity if you are to be honest with students about what you can really offer them. The aim is to develop strategies appropriate to a particular student's own style of working; suggestions of different approaches and techniques for students to try out must remain as suggestions, with control lying in the student's hands.

For the study counsellor there can be a desire to give in to temptation and try prescribing a technique in the face of a person's severe anxiety, not least because we are likely to share some of the emotions they express as adult learners. To do so is to reinforce a student's lack of confidence by indicating that control lies in your hands, and to confirm that there are mysteries of study to which only a few have access. There are parallels with other counselling relationships, and McLoughlin (1990: 60–1) has described the need to acknowledge boundaries:

> I believe that recognising limitations is essential. For example, even if the client wants me to cure him or her, as a counsellor I must know and acknowledge that I am unable to do so. What I can do is genuinely co-operate with the client in a relationship which consistently and for a period of time seeks to uncover hidden patterns and influences which beset the client's life. By doing this, relief of symptoms, changes in behaviour and deeper self-understandings become possible.

'Hidden patterns and influences' shape the nature of study problems, especially writing, as much as they do other aspects of life. By providing time and a safe space for those in need to explore study-related matters more deeply there is a chance for students to take back control of their intellectual selves and to gain confidence by negotiating new challenges.

Myths and assumptions

Study counselling is substantially taken up with helping students to foster what Rowntree has described as the ability to reflect on their own academic experiences rather than searching for the one correct way to study. A reflective student has a sense of purpose, can develop strategies to meet their own as well as institutional requirements, and understands the situation in which they are working (Rowntree 1991: 6). Aiding students in their quests to become effectively reflective requires one to be aware of the impact of the myths and fantasies which surround degree-level education. One dominant myth is that good students 'naturally' know how to study, so the matter needs no discussion. This makes my work that of a tour guide, encouraging students to make sense of the curious, unexplained customs and habits of their temporary environment.

Admitting to working as a study counsellor can lead to raised eyebrows and disdain for all that sort of unpleasantness thought to have crept in during the 1980s. Eyebrow-raisers often believe that able students already know all they need to about study, so to have problems or to examine how you study is, of itself, a sign of lack of ability. To engage openly in teaching students about study is seen as a sign of these bedevilled times, of lowered standards, and to be distinctly *déclassé*. Talking about 'skills' raises strong emotions in those who see all academic teaching as fostering innate intelligence, and therefore sees an understanding of the education system as irrelevant to intellectual endeavour.

It is easy to assume that all new students understand the basics about what universities do and how they go about their work. This is not so, but nor is it always the case for some academic staff and counsellors as they move around from short-term job to short-term job, travelling to gain expertise and promotion, experiencing different institutions and different approaches to degrees. For students, one helpful question to learn to ask of themselves is: 'What do I know already?' In counselling, when concentrating on any aspect of study, it is the question which will stay with people so that, in the future, when faced with new academic challenges, they always have a starting point. So stepping-stones to answering this are the following basic questions:

- What is a 'degree'?
- Where is it taught?
- How is it taught?
- Describe those teaching methods in detail.

Looking at the context in this way is about starting to ask what is expected of students rather than making unquestioned assumptions. It is not unusual to hear people say something like 'Of course, I'm not a real student', and the first step to understanding this is to find out what their assumed image of a 'real student' is. If they differ substantially from that, are they better or worse, more skilled or less skilled? What skills would they like to acquire, and how could they go about getting them? The answer to this last question often provides a useful means of setting up an agreed agenda for student and study counsellor collaboration.

One problem that can manifest itself quite early when considering context and expectations in this way is the realization that all a student's ambitions are off in the future – for example, what they will have to offer employers on graduation. If there is little of interest to students apart from gaining a degree, then they face a long and painful three or four years as undergraduates; some interim aims need to be considered.

The sense of not being a 'real student' is an expression, usually, of not being quite good enough. While there are occasional people who mean that they see other students as inferior, most view their fellow students as super-able. To begin to move away from this global sense of dissatisfaction, counsellors can help students establish what skills they think they ought to develop to be *competent* students. I am always conscious that comparing oneself to others encourages an existing tendency to self-abasement, so the inherent comparison in this approach is not satisfactory. However, it does have the advantage of making academic work become more accessible and attainable. As it becomes clearer that study does not occur by osmosis, and that skills can be developed self-consciously, then it can help to become even more specific, and analyse undergraduate tasks according to the skills they demand. This exercise needs to be tailored to individual students, concentrating on those tasks they are asked to do. For tutors who wish to open up this debate with students, a necessary preparation is to work out one's own thoughts, as laid out in Exercise 2.1, about the types of skills required to carry out academic tasks.

Exercise 2.1 is about understanding the most basic elements of university life. This serves two purposes. One is to help students share knowledge and ensure that simple questions are answered without a need to make public admissions of ignorance. The second, for staff, is to practise explaining the basics to other people. Staff may think they know about these issues and have nothing to say on them. However, if people are going to learn to listen to students' expectations and if they are going to teach others, then counsellors and tutors need to learn to put into words which are comprehensible and brief those matters which are usually taken for granted.

Exercise 2.1: Skills

What specific skills do students need to deal with?

Lectures	Essays	Lab/experiment reports
Seminars	Reports	Field work
Examinations	Projects	Tutorials

Students, like staff, believe myths about natural ability. The commonest one is reflected in the student boast that they never do any academic work.

The gentlemanly 2ii has a long history and has crossed continents. Steinberg (1974) has written of how, in nineteenth-century American universities, one objection to Jewish students was their tendency to work hard and get high marks. To make matters worse, they got good degrees in such unpleasant subjects as engineering. No one (well, not many) openly objected to their being Jewish, it was just their lack of manners, their serious intent in study and what was judged to be their ghastly bad taste in subjects.

Perish the thought that at this end of the twentieth century we might have remnants of similar ideas. Persuading students that working steadily is not a sign of stupidity is something I spend a lot of time doing. Persuading them that working secretly is not necessary in a university seems an odd way to earn a living. However, the myth that real ability comes naturally, requires little fostering and even less work is one which dies hard.

Graduates also subscribe to this fantasy: it is the nudge-nudge, wink-wink variety of reminiscences. This is about graduates' daydreams: the notion that in late adolescence we were let loose from nice homes, free and with money to spend long summer days doing little apart from the odd bit of punting or copulating. Of course, no work was done, but one still managed to fly through examinations with ease. This tale has a double-edged effect: first, to show the listener that we did not engage in anything as swotty and nasty as work; and second, to show that one is naturally so brilliant that a 2ii came easily. What might have happened had we turned our rapier brains seriously to academic work? It is perhaps graduates' fantasies which stop people outside universities understanding that 1930s images of Oxford and Cambridge have little bearing on conditions today. Barry Hughill (1993) described this romanticism as stemming from the television adaptation of Waugh's *Brideshead Revisited*, in an article in which he catalogues the reality of student poverty. Day-to-day life in universities rarely gets acknowledged in a world ridden with clichés about 'ivory towers'. The amnesia, which rapidly forgets the manifold truths about undergraduate life, makes it hard for us to hear apparently successful students as they try to express distress about their work, their abilities or their futures.

Few students, in fact, have a clue what they are working towards. What good academic work looks like is an unknown factor. Developing the capacity to reflect on the structure as well as the content of set texts as a way of discovering what desirable work looks like is rarely encouraged as an integral part of most courses. Discovering new strategies for meeting academic challenges is not a commonplace approach at degree level; the focus is rather on ability. Assumptions are unthinkingly made about the progress students ought to make, hence any hiccups become problematized. The notion that some people are academically able while others lack the mental capacity for study leads to inflating the difficulties faced and to getting them out of perspective, for if every problem is experienced as a sign that one should not be an undergraduate then minor problems can easily become major crises. Stumbling along the way, asking too many questions, asking them in the wrong way, not progressing at the required pace are all seen, by students as well as staff, as signs of inability. Teaching those who are already attuned to degree-level expectations on arrival, who can more easily pick up cues about what good work looks like, is the easy part of teaching. Problems arise when teaching able people who do not, for whatever reasons, share or comprehend your values, and will not be attuned until and unless those values are made explicit.

All education systems reflect assumptions about knowledge, and one benefit of travelling to foreign universities is to learn new approaches. Whatever individual experiences and expectations we bring to learning, as students we still have to adjust and adapt to a social institution with its own codes. Yet students who try to define what it is they are working towards are in danger of being seen as incapable. For we are somewhat ingenuous and insist that it is individual analysis and argument which gain approval and marks, and to ask about the nature of the end-product is taken to show a lack of ability and initiative of itself. Our confusion is expressed when we describe students rather than their work as 'first class', where others get third-class degrees. Similarly muddled thinking surrounds access to degrees for students with disabilities: we have become used to 'letting in' blind, wheelchair-bound, aged students, and many institutions now make loud noises about their openness. However, universities were not designed primarily for the physically impaired, and whatever good intentions exist such students may well find themselves using service lifts and back routes, past dustbins and through car parks. The design reflects our underlying assumption that degrees are really for young, fit people; and, looking at any crowd of undergraduates, they are usually white as well. We are not clear what constitutes disability: is it anything that impairs the development and expression of intellectual ability; or is it anything which impinges on an image of the first-class student as young, male, fit (two arms, two legs and no dribbling, please), white, and able to get high marks without causing the institution any trouble?

Few people are so overtly crass in their expectations of students, yet Hurst's study of the reality of access for people with physical disabilities (which did not include problems of sight or hearing) led him to conclude that there is still a need for changes in the ideology of an institution, its staff and its curriculum to avoid problems even when there is a more egalitarian belief that individuals should be enabled to take up what is theirs by right (Hurst 1993: 355–6). Paradoxically, changes in attitudes may be less problematic for teaching departments in cases of obvious disability, such as the use of an amanuensis in examinations for blind students. When the case does not appear to the observer to be easily defined as disability, then there are mutterings about fairness and cheating. Questions arise about what it is essential for students to do to complete a degree successfully and what is not, with temperatures rising. Where, for example, do you stand on the issue of officially acknowledging specific learning difficulties (commonly known as 'dyslexia')? The problem goes something like this: your department has agreed to a series of concessions for a student who has an acceptable statement of dyslexia; once these concessions have been allowed, the student is gaining first-class marks. How do you feel about that situation?

Assumptions, when examined, can turn out to be valid educational philosophies of which one could be proud. But when hidden or unexamined, it is possible for social mores to masquerade as criteria of excellence. Writing the traditional essay embodies cultural dilemmas for home-based as well as overseas students, because it is the means of being socialized into disciplinary approaches as well as providing a basis for assessment. The greatest individual work is believed to be the PhD, and supervisors want to recruit students who have individual flair, ability and the capacity to think for themselves. But you must think for yourself within the framework of an existing discipline and its current trends, for there is little mileage in presenting a thesis ten years too early or ten years too late. As my (fourth) supervisor explained with refreshing honesty, you have to do as teacher says but you must also have something to say yourself. There may be sound educational reasons for this, but thinking for yourself while fitting in is not precisely the same as thinking for yourself.

If staff have not examined their own assumptions then it is difficult to find the means to enable students to overcome challenges. So when postgraduates, in frustration, demand to know what they have to do to get a PhD, they may well get a frosty reception. Likewise students who ask how their essay could have become a first-class essay. The questioner and questioned can misunderstand each other disastrously. Students cannot understand the wishy-washy 'well, we know a first when we see it' sort of response, suspecting that it hides an assessment of the person, not the work. Staff can become concerned that they are faced with students who have not got the ability to think for themselves, and want to gain degrees in a 'painting by numbers' manner.

When teaching staff have little awareness or interest in study matters they are often quite happy to have these taken off their hands by technical staff coming in to teach students about study. There are others who have the humanitarian desire to help what they perceive to be weaker students by providing study specialists. Embedded in both these attitudes is the assumption that study is about the objective application of a set of techniques which can somehow be separated out from both students and the course content, and so be delivered in a disembodied form. And there is a lot which students can be taught about study. First, they need to understand that they should always review how they go about their work, reflecting on how helpful, appropriate or fun their approach is. It is not a matter of waiting for a 'study problem' to appear; and nor is it a matter of learning 'how to do' study once and for ever. Rather, what you learn and how you learn it, what you put into academic work and what you get out varies throughout your entire life. How you work and what you want from academic thought should be different at 15 than it is at 50. Change is part of learning; facing new challenges and developing new strategies for overcoming them is a part of intellectual growth.

Academic development, however, does grind to a halt. Whatever the good intentions, no matter how excellent the teaching or motivated the students, there are times when everything known about study seems to vaporize. Students suddenly find themselves with a backlog of work, a pile of untouched good intentions and unmet deadlines, and to have run out of excuses. In the next chapter I look at 'first meetings' and what happens as dispirited students approach tutor/counsellors against this institutional backdrop, with all its spoken and unspoken expectations.

3

Tell Me About It: First Meetings

Introduction

First meetings are times when students define their academic problems and describe what they do, why they are doing it, how they came to do it and how they go about studying. This 'setting of the scene' is a precursor to devising strategies which suit an individual student's needs, situation and style of study. Even better if it leads to students devising their own strategies. Students defining their own problems is the vital process, the means by which they begin to take some control and grow in academic confidence. It is not a matter-of-fact prelude before the 'expert' takes over ownership of the situation by providing a diagnosis. First meetings take place, usually, when students are up against a serious deadline or a crunch period of some kind. Their patience is not always great, and study counsellors come under pressure to diagnose and prescribe correct techniques which can then be applied three times a day, after meals.

It is fair to say that I carry certain expectations of first meetings, of points I hope to have worked towards by the end of the first session, if it has seemed appropriate. My hopes, like those of students, can be hopelessly over-ambitious, and may only be achieved by the time we come to the end of many meetings. Hence, reviewing how a particular 'case' is going includes assessing the continued relevance of one's own expectations and the extent to which they are or are not being met, and whether they are getting in the way of a student's progress. Tutor/counsellors should examine their own expectations: it does happen that, from time to time, we lose patience with a student who appears not to make progress. It can be that the student concerned is quite happy and feels that highly satisfactory changes have occurred. The sin committed is that the student has not performed according to the study tutor's unexamined expectations of the counselling process, and hence personal sense of success in the job. My list for first meetings is something like this:

1. I hope to understand better what is troubling the student.
2. I hope to get a picture of the context in which this problem has arisen – an understanding of the student's route to this moment in time.
3. A part of that context is how the student has previously experienced being taught, so I hope to get some idea of how they have enjoyed school, college or other formal teaching.
4. To gain a sense of the student's hopes and expectations about study and about university life – what they want from courses.
5. All of this is part of starting the student on the path to defining their own situation. I hope to release some expression of this control during the first meeting.
6. I would like to finish a first meeting with an idea of what we might focus on in further meetings if these are required, so that both the student and I have agreed an agenda, however loose.
7. I want the student to leave with a sense of comfort, of having been heard in safety and cared for in a welcoming environment, to go with some stirrings of confidence.
8. At the end of a session, I expect to have ideas about which areas are sensitive and difficult for the student. Although we may not necessarily discuss them directly, what I offer will be informed and shaped by understanding the wider picture of the student's life.

This is not a blueprint laying out how sessions should be conducted. My list of preferences is just one ingredient in a meeting which should be characterized by the study counsellor's ability to be responsive to the student's needs. My way of practising says that you must start from wherever the student is. Starting with the student's definition of the problem, responding to their needs. Sometimes this can be a request for basic information such as: how long essays should be, whom to see about financial problems, or understanding how to use commas. It can be more profound matters, such as taking risks when writing essays. It is easy to say that a study counsellor starts from where a student is, but much harder to do, not least because a large part of the problem is that students often do not know where they are. The process of enabling students to define their academic situation is hard work, not easy to achieve, and immensely beneficial to students. To define where you are is the first step in learning to take responsibility for your own academic work, and hence working independently, achieving the satisfaction of meeting internal standards rather than just depending on the views of external assessors.

All 'first meetings' in a counselling service can be difficult, as can students' first tentative approaches to tutors for help. With study there is the added pressure of time: whatever you believe a tutor/counsellor should do, the student is usually right up against serious deadlines. What causes the student to arrive at your door shapes the tenor of the first minutes. Some people come because they have been advised to seek help, others come because, unhelpfully, they have been told that they *must* seek your help. How this referral has been made can set up a first meeting to be even more difficult than usual if it has undermined the confidence of students or taken away their choices. They may have tried everything else. Most students feel ashamed when seeking help and academic work could well be the only area of life which has, apparently, been successfully dealt with up to now. For students with physical disabilities there is the daunting prospect of explaining to yet another person exactly what their disabilities are and what this implies for completing a degree. Then there are other students who know full well that study is the tip of their personal iceberg, and academic problems seem safer to look at. Even answering questions about what subjects they are studying can be treated as if the study counsellor is asking grossly personal questions. Each new arrival has mentally conjured up a study expert who fits in with personal notions of academic work and what constitutes study or intellectual life.

Getting started

I start by saying something banal, like 'Tell me what's been happening.' I suspect that what is said matters very little, that in those first minutes it is the unspoken conversation that decides how much someone is prepared to divulge. I suffer from a sort of stage-fright at this point. In the past I put this down to meeting students not in a room of my own but on borrowed territory. I am not referring here to the academic mania for requiring your own 'home from home'. Rather, there is an uncomfortable dishonesty in being surrounded by other people's books, pictures and paraphernalia, and a newly encountered student will examine these closely while they decide whether or not you are trustworthy. I always wanted to confess my fraudulence, but first meetings with unhappy people are not appropriate moments for discussing housekeeping or employment matters. Apart from which, chattering interrupts that peculiar telepathy which confirms your trustworthiness or untrustworthiness, independent of whether you have just spilt the coffee or tripped over your bootlaces. McLoughlin (1990: 58) has described how his analyst's 'impact as a person' was as important as his therapeutic behaviour, and now, in his own practice, finds the memory of this highly personal impact helpful in keeping the 'expert' in him under control. While I hope to be of help to people, I am also conscious that this is a personal relationship, and it is the person I am who is trying to help.

More important than my shyness is the client's nervousness. They are in unknown territory, physically and mentally, about to confess problems to a stranger. I prefer to start slowly, by saying something suitably vague so that if people's minds are full of their nearest and dearest having kicked them out that morning, I am not rabbiting on about something inappropriate, invasive. Suitably vague – such as 'So, tell me what's been happening' – so that the student can start defining the situation.

Well there isn't anything to say really.
I wish I hadn't come.
It's all so stupid.
I should be able to sort it out for myself.
I'm probably just being stupid.
I think there must be something wrong with me.
It's nothing really.
Everyone else copes.
There isn't anything to say.
Just give me some handouts.
It's the exams.
I haven't got time to talk.
I'm behind with my essays.
I can never remember anything.
Are you qualified?
My tutor says I can't write essays properly.
I've got this backlog, I've written it all down.
Just phone my tutor and explain for me.
They said I should talk to you.
Do you know anything about doing a degree?
I don't think there's anything you can do to help me.
I can't get the reading done.
I can't write.
I'm wasting your time.
My tutor says I'm dyslexic.
I'm sure there are people with worse problems than mine.
I think there's something wrong with my head.

Responding

Like all academics, I always believe that I am responding to words. Usually words about academic matters are translated into print or written down, but occasionally we will settle for the spoken word. But of course, so much else goes on, to which we respond wittingly or unwittingly. I rarely think about being an undergraduate, but if I am honest there are occasions when I have caught myself looking at students' faces and thinking: 'Was I like that?' Whatever bizarre process leads me to think that, it is a sign that I am not really listening to the student – for with study there is a great danger that you are, unawares, comparing a student's experience with your own. As counsellors or tutors in higher education, we have all studied, though we have not all experienced violence or other events in students' lives. As long as the student's experience is beyond our own, it can be clearer where the counsellor begins and the client ends. To help students with study it is vital that as study counsellors we have high levels of insight into our own experiences of academic work and academic environments, but that is not the same as using past experience as a touchstone while students are trying to unravel their thoughts. As with other aspects of life, the time to develop insight into yourself is before meeting students, not while they are struggling to make sense of their worlds.

Some people are hunched, look down, women use their hair as a curtain, people sit on the edges of comfortable armchairs, refusing to let go. An offer to take someone's jacket can be met as if it were the start of an assault. Otherwise cool and composed people embarrass themselves by bursting into tears at the mention of academic work. As a tutor, there can be a feeling of rising panic: we should be able to come up with a technique, a way out, an answer, especially if there is pressure to meet students' deadlines. Come up with an answer now, just to prove your worth, show me that you are really fit for this job, turn water into wine and prove it to me. As academics we think we are listening just because we are not talking, and study is about teaching; a request for help can elicit teaching mode, and teaching mode is about instructing, talking. Listening is not about talking, nor is it just committing the supreme sacrifice of shutting up when you are tempted into teaching mode, talking mode. Empathic listening is not about repeating back a few words spoken by students, rather it is an active process of entering into that person's world. Rogers (1967: 73) described empathy in relation to a client:

> Can I step into his private world so completely that I lose all desire to evaluate or judge it? Can I enter it so sensitively that I can move about in it freely, without trampling on meanings which are precious to him? Can I sense it so accurately that I can catch not only those meanings of his experience which are obvious to him, but those meanings which are only implicit, which he sees only dimly or as confusion?

Power lies with the person who defines. The tutor/counsellor's job is to help students define their situations, including the confusion, and to explore that which, up until now, has only been dimly known or half-sensed.

> Tell me about it.
> How can I help?
> What made you come today?
> How are you feeling today?
> What's the situation?
> When you say 'behind', can you tell me a bit more about what that
>   means?
> Tell me about the essays.
> Tell me about your courses.
> What's been happening this term?
> Do you know how it all came about?
> Tell me what the problem is.
> You sound very worried.
> And how do you feel about it?
> What do you think is happening?

Explaining the situation to a stranger can help. It is a cliché, but having someone listen with care and kindness (empathy is hard at the beginning) really does make a difference. Having an hour set aside just for you, to be taken seriously and treated kindly, is a balm which not only soothes but also increases the confidence to go back out and try again with a challenging situation. Away from the department which marks and assesses you, sets the work, sets the deadlines and exercises power over academic life and death, a counselling service can provide an environment which ensures no interruptions. This alone is difficult anywhere else in universities, where meetings are ever imminent, telephones ring, doors are always knocked on, and there is the permanent, restless, tramping of feet up and down corridors. In some teaching departments only professors are permitted to switch their telephones through to secretarial staff, and telephone systems are designed to noisily grab attention. Hence, interruptions are guaranteed for the least convenient moment, often just as students are beginning to describe problems in detail.

So students lurk in the corridors, trying to set up meetings with elusive staff. When they get to meet them, it is not clear how long is allowed for the meeting. How much is their entitlement? How much help are they fairly allowed? A counselling service should, at least, allow time, space and some self-respect. The atmosphere ought to be peaceful and quiet, away from the confusion of busy institutions, and students should carry away with them an impression of warmth and kindness. Everywhere else people will have told them how to deal with study problems, and they have already failed to make use of a long list of advice, so counsellors must think hard before rushing to add to this catalogue of failure.

It is easy to jump to hasty conclusions with study problems. But as with all listening, assuming that you know what it is all about, diagnostically wrapping up a student's study crisis in your own answers, is a highly effective way of closing down communication. What Ford and Merriman (1990: 17) have called 'blinkered ears', that capacity to stereotype and categorize within minutes of beginning to listen to a client, works against listening openly. Dass and Gorman (1985: 99) see these judgements as the means by which we preselect and listen less, as one thought cancels out another. They write of how one's state of mind can transcend transient states, such as tiredness: the mind's potential for awareness of itself is, they argue, what offers help and healing, and to be with an 'open, quiet, playful, receptive, or reflective' mind is to experience supportiveness (1985: 94). The process of listening Dass and Gorman describe requires a particular mental discipline: to hear, to be aware, to know one's own responses to what is said, but not to chase every thought distractedly, instead to focus quietly on the situation and the person in need (see, particularly, 1985: 91–118). There is, then, a delicate balance to be struck, because as a tutor/counsellor you will have heard similar stories before, but as long as you are analysing and diagnosing then you are not listening in a way which helps students release their own feelings. By taking over professional ownership of study crises, one is excluding students from the process of developing strategies to meet challenges.

Confidentiality matters, knowing that what you say is private. Being able to admit to stupidity, failure, fear, doubts, all without assessors, referees, fellow students or the world knowing. It is the bus-stop situation, talking to someone who is not part of your life, has no axe to grind and whom you never have to see again. That works for study as much as for other aspects of life. Sadly, not all the world sees it that way. Departments often see study as being about lack of ability, therefore an assessment/teaching matter without much emotional impact. So the word 'confidential' at the top of a letter from me might be taken as an invitation to photocopy and circulate round all the teaching staff of a department. I have even seen a memo summarizing a staff member's conversation with an unhappy student, photocopied complete with teacher's diagnosis. Privacy is important, and it beats ritual humiliation any day.

Students may arrive in a panic because someone in authority has told them that they might be dyslexic. Being told you have a specific learning difficulty, as dyslexia is now known to be, implies, for many people, a specific set of responses. If the word 'dyslexic' does not instantly say everything that is necessary, some students will doubt that you know your job. However, the exact collection of symptoms which comes under the heading of 'dyslexia' varies from person to person, as does their severity, and will have a greater or lesser effect depending on the student's course. At this stage, how a student feels about themselves substantially shapes how they respond to the tag 'dyslexic'. Students with severe dyslexia have usually held discussions about likely problems and what the institution can offer at the time of admission. Those who have been 'statemented' while at school are often phlegmatic about the whole business, with years of experience of how to manage. While they may consult a tutor/counsellor when adapting to academic demands in a new environment, one can learn much about study by listening to them. In my experience, being diagnosed as dyslexic for the first time while an undergraduate constitutes a personal crisis.

Mature students especially, meeting the word for the first time, can feel their whole world crumble. At the same time as perhaps having changed direction in life completely when registering to study for a degree, they discover that they are deeply flawed. Or, at least, that is how it is experienced: as a sign that there is something significantly wrong in the brain which is going to stop them graduating. Being told that their learning problems come under the title of 'dyslexia' is experienced as confirming what was learnt in childhood, that they are not the sort of person who can do academic work. For people who respond in this way, being allowed concessions, such as extra time in examinations, feels like they are cheating and being given something which is not their right. Putting back the pieces and becoming more flexible in one's thought about what constitutes 'academic' is more urgent work with such students than attempting to teach new study techniques, for as long as the distress lasts a study counsellor's pearls of wisdom will be unheard.

Another fear which goes along with the sense of being diminished is that this diagnosis will interfere with job prospects, and hopes for the future. When meeting for the first time, students may well be angry as well as distressed, ashamed and disappointed.

What is not comfortable for a study counsellor is to act as the meat in the sandwich: to be a referral agent only, who has to send students onwards to a psychologist for testing because powerful people elsewhere insist on this, and then watch all these other implications crash in when it is too late for the student to have any choices or chances to discuss the implications of testing.

Defining: values and motivation

Education is something that many of us have had done to us. Taking responsibility for it and learning to work independently starts with trying to describe our intellectual life to an interested listener. Few of us are aware that we have our own academic fingerprint. Instead, we desperately search for the correct ways of doing things, from study skills manuals, from fellow students, from lecturers. All these are excellent sources for new ideas, but only to adapt and to incorporate into what we do already. First meetings are about trying to get a picture of students' academic fingerprints: what problems they are faced with, why they are doing what they do, how they came to do it and how they go about studying – from writing and reading through to taking lecture notes.

M: Tell me what you like about (your subject).

S: I dunno, what do you mean?

M: I just wondered what made it attractive to you.

S: Nothing really, I couldn't do anything else.

M: What were the choices?

S: Well, I thought about doing astronomy, but I struggled with it and the teacher changed halfway through, and I only got a C for it. And aeronautics, well I got an A for it but you can only really do it to A level, to do it any further you'd have needed to do chemistry as well, only I didn't know that when I started.

M: You sound a bit disappointed.

S: Yeah. I don't know what I expected. I was disappointed with my A-level results really, I only got an A, a B and a C, and everyone else is quite bright. I wanted to go to university, I wanted to get away. What else can you do? I couldn't have got a job, but I'm not sure I'm up to scratch.

As teachers, as counsellors and as students we all have set ideas about what is good and bad motivation towards study. Our social values include acceptable reasons for studying, and we look down on people who do not share those social values. So those who view degrees as about personal enhancement and academic enrichment often have little time for those who see degrees as passports to well-paid jobs. Students who expect a course to be training for a specific career or profession will waste little energy on what are perceived to be the more esoteric or abstract elements. Tutors who intend helping students need to think about which reasons for study they like or dislike, for you will not help someone frustrated by lack of deep thought in their course if you, the tutor, are irritated when courses are not practically orientated. Likewise, you will not be able to help students on courses which you assume are 'practical' if you believe that all applied courses in universities should be abolished because their students are not up to scratch. Exercise 3.1 is a simple way for tutors to consider these issues.

Exercise 3.1: Why go to university?

Write down a reason which describes why you went to university.

Come up with three more reasons why other people might decide to go to university. These reasons should be as different to your thinking as possible.

Go through the list and think about what you like and dislike about each reason for starting a degree, including your own.

If on a staff development course and the group atmosphere feels appropriate, I would present the group with a list of reasons for undertaking a degree and ask them to state which reasons they approve of and why, and which they do not like and why. It is better to discover you have set ideas about 'healthy' reasons for studying and to explore what your beliefs are *before* you meet students in need of your help. Academic staff as well as students have strong responses to words like 'science' and 'arts': even in universities there are people who see science as the shallow reproduction from memory of known and established facts; and there are others who view arts students as left-wing dabblers in waffly, ivory-tower theories.

Many students have, according to the rest of the world, done very well academically. They usually have excellent entry qualifications or prior experience. Yet still they find ways to define their prior successes as failures. I am aware that sometimes I am called upon to be useless, and am just a part of a wrangle between two or more people. It goes something like this. If an appointment with me is kept, then it is possible to say: 'You see, I tried everything, I even went to see the study woman, and it was all useless.' This is rarely done intentionally, and is part of a person's wider relationship with success and failure. The process by which occasional students commit themselves to failure is not straightforward and should be broached by tutor/counsellors with great care. Ideally, I would prefer people to experience academic success and failure as choices rather than to feel driven to courses of behaviour over which students perceive themselves to have little control.

First meetings can rarely get deeply into such sensitive areas. But you can begin to get echoes of these larger issues as you start to explore what students hope will come out of meeting you, and what you are aiming for together:

What would you like to see happen?
If it were an entirely free world, how would you like things to be?
What would you like us to concentrate on in these sessions?

The answers to these questions depend on confidentiality and are hard for students to answer. They are questions to be repeated during later sessions as students grow in confidence and are clearer about what they feel comfortable asking of you. What people would like the world to look like can, on occasion, be far removed from being a student studying their chosen subjects. In which case:

That's quite different to what you're doing now, how do you feel about that gulf?
How do you get from where you are now to that sort of situation?

Students may just want some support from you while they grit their teeth and finish the last months of a much-hated course. Maybe they need to think seriously about how long teeth-gritting can be sustained, if they are just at the beginning of a degree. Either way, the answers will imply a quite different input from a counsellor or tutor.

At this stage people can be anxious to let you know how stupid they are compared with their qualifications, that their past successes mean little. Yet, paradoxically, they can still be covering up what they perceive to be the true depth of their inability and stupidity. The internal picture can be one of a blot on the landscape, while the external picture projected is of a lucky, over-marked student. Rather than accepting good marks as a fair reflection of the work completed, given the constraints of academic criteria, people tie themselves in knots trying to sustain a belief in their stupidity. Instead of accepting their competence, students will make comments about the outside world which are intended to undermine the validity of the judgement passed on their academic performance. The following are commonly heard ways of maintaining the status quo:

Well, it's only Lowtown University. You wouldn't get marks like these at Oxford/Cambridge/ . . . .
It's only a college, it's not a real university.
That tutor's well known for being a soft marker.
I think he/she felt sorry for me.
It's not a very good department, so they do give good marks easily.
They're just trying to encourage us.
It's not a very good year/group, so my work looks better than it is.
He/she is new, so he/she's not used to marking yet.
I was on form that day/week/month/year.

I was lucky with the questions.

Lots of people got through, it was easy that year/month/week.

Of course, I chose easy subjects.

It may have been a good mark, but I had to work harder/longer than everyone else to get it.

There was a lot of flu/black death/colds around at the time, so I was lucky I wasn't ill like other people.

I'd done that topic before, it's not like it was new to me.

I got a lot of help for that one, a lot of guidance.

I just know how to play the system, that's all.

Achieving good academic standards is not always as desirable as it might first appear to onlookers as consistent success requires too big a change in how students see themselves, breaking down the belief in stupidity. The word 'academic' can conjure up unattractive characteristics. During a counselling session it is possible to ask something like: 'This word "academic" means such different things to different people, tell me what it means to you?' If students are confused by the question, often not having considered it explicitly before, a way of helping is to pick up a pencil and say something like: 'Well, if you were to write a list of words describing what "academic" means, what would be on your list?' Another variation, as you are working towards including a more positive approach is to write a 'good' list and a 'bad' list: what are the good things about having an academic approach, and what are the bad things? Sometimes the list remains resolutely bleak, so after exploring that emptiness it can help to say: 'Well, those are the bad aspects of the word "academic", what are the good aspects?' If they cannot see any good aspects to being academic then maybe the discussion should be moving on, delicately, to why people are engaging in an activity in which they can see no good whatsoever. But if you still wish to pursue the 'good' list, then: 'Well, what might others see as good about the word "academic"?'

Why students are committing an enormous amount of energy to achieving something they see as undesirable is a matter which must be considered, but perhaps not always broached directly in the first meeting. Defining the whole exercise as worthless is a way of ensuring that we do not grow in confidence as work meets with success, according to external marking. Seeing the marks for what they are worth is not the same as saying that the whole system is corrupt and empty, that the student receiving high marks merely knows how to manipulate the system. Facing up to yourself as capable and bright is highly threatening to many students, and a study counsellor who really wants to help needs to learn how to challenge destructive self-assessments in academic work as well as more generally in life.

Counsellors, too, can share with students a fear, dislike or a disdain for academic values. A straight divide is assumed between the academic and the emotional, leading to a view that to be academic is to be unreal, unauthentic, ungenuine and to escape from your emotional life. In order to help students be aware of their assumptions about intellectual life, so that they can stretch the boundaries, we need, first, to gain some insight and awareness of our own responses to intellectual activity. Quite rightly, counselling courses concentrate on ensuring that potential counsellors develop emotional self-awareness, and redress professionals' emphasis on detachment and diagnosis by making students examine their own lives and emotions. However, this does not mean that intellectual development does not matter, or that we can confirm our own academic values by insisting that life is a simple, dualistic, choice between the intellect and the emotions. That lack of insight means we have a vested interest in students denying their own academic values. While many may wish, ultimately, to deny what they define as academic, there are many more students who do not wish to, who subscribe to those sorts of values and wish to achieve intellectually. That is why study problems matter to them. It is no help to them if the tutor/counsellor is, at heart, cynical about the whole enterprise.

Contracts

To help students grow in confidence and take control of the situation, it is important that they know what to expect from me, at least by jointly agreeing or outlining the likely number of meetings and possible themes to be addressed. Yet, however desirable, it is hard in first meetings to negotiate a schedule of future meetings, for some students find that meeting a particular crisis is a sufficient confidence-booster for them. Some like an 'open-door' arrangement whereby they can, from time to time, check in to talk about how study is progressing rather than waiting until a crisis builds up. Others cannot address the wider study problems which have got them into a mess until the crisis has passed, and then we can arrange to meet a certain number of times, and agree an agenda between us. Only when they have gone away, tried new ideas, experienced new successes and thought about our meetings do students decide what suits them, which can lead to cancelled and rescheduled appointments, changes of mind or new suggestions for work when we do meet. However, I am highly conscious that waiting until the student feels confident enough to dictate our programme of work can give an impression of powerfulness on my part with which I am most uncomfortable. Grierson (1990: 30) has described a similar situation when meeting with a counsellor:

> I was also rather mixed up about what was supposed to be happening in the relationship between us. There was no contract or discussion about what was appropriate during these meetings and no money was involved. My rights in the relationship were not discussed and no time was specified for each session nor how many sessions I could expect to have. It was scary and I felt uncertain about the future commitment of the counsellor.

By not establishing clear boundaries a tutor/counsellor can give out the opposite messages to those intended, encouraging bewilderment and a sense that the counsellor is not really interested and does not care what happens next. However, as Mearns and Dryden (1990: 126) argue, clients are often too vulnerable in first meetings to establish a once-and-for-ever contract, rather one must negotiate and renegotiate, restate and clarify what is being offered, and reassure that it will go on being offered. What is not helpful is for the institution to lay down how many meetings are permitted as a means of managing limited resources, and Mearns and Thorne (1988: 111) have pointed out that this merely takes power from both client and counsellor, whatever claims are made for therapeutic efficacy. Some students benefit from only one or two sessions, in which case an upper limit is irrelevant. For those who need more than the maximum permitted time, then all the effort has been wasted if the work cannot continue beyond the institution's time limit. For me, the end of a first meeting is often a summary, whereby I can check out if I have really understood what the student is hoping for, and if I have made clear what I can offer; sometimes we might make a skeleton plan for future action.

> M: It sounds as if your marks have been very good when you are writing. Am I right in understanding that you want to get less wound up when you're writing?
> S: Yeah, sort of. Like, it takes too long. Life's too short.
> M: OK. So you'd like us to think about ways of cutting back the time spent – is it just on writing, or is it the reading as well?
> S: It's all of it, I just get so worried, I don't know what to leave in, what to take out. I get so worried taking notes from books, I have reams of notes.
> M: Right. So selection is an issue. How would it be if we met next week and the week after to think about those issues, and then we can stop and think again about how things are going?

Ideally, I want students to leave first meetings with a sense of having been heard, and knowing that while the problems facing them are difficult, they are manageable even if we do not have the exact answers immediately to hand. Life is rarely this easy, but a loose contract in the early stages is preferable to having no agreement about future plans whatsoever, which leaves students with little sense of what they are entitled to ask for or to expect. It leaves them with the same sense of helplessness which they experience when haunting departmental corridors looking for members of academic staff. Most importantly, the lost feeling experienced is not a firm basis on which to build the kind of relationship within which, one hopes, students feel sufficiently safe to explore hitherto frightening problems.

First meetings, then, are about getting to know one another and setting the scene. Students get a glimpse of what the tutor/counsellor might offer, and should feel heard, understood and safe. Having spent time in a comfortable, relaxed environment, I hope that they also go away feeling comforted and a little more confident. Whatever the external pressures of time and deadlines, the process of students learning to take control of their study crises should have begun. The tutor/counsellor and the student will have a clearer picture of the context in which study problems have arisen: why that subject matters to the student, how they came to choose it, how they have (or have not) enjoyed learning in the past and what they hope for from undergraduate studies. From this personal picture, a study counsellor will be in a better position to help a student develop ways of overcoming current challenges and will have picked up echoes of which wider issues surround study for the individual concerned. In the next chapter I look at ways of moving gently into some of these more difficult areas as they impact on study.

4

Talking 1: Aims and Expectations

How are you?

Tutor/counsellors try to help students to talk. To talk, that is, in a directed and constructive way, helping them to knit into a coherent pattern those disjointed, painful responses to the business of learning which are hampering progress. Taking the half-glimpsed prior experiences of education, the current frustrations of undergraduate life and the shamefaced hopes for the future, and helping students make sense of the whole so that it becomes a more constructive and dynamic pool of personal resources for individuals to draw on.

It is easy to be businesslike about academic work, to keep to a schedule agreed with a student, and to become infected by the view that academic work is a dispassionate matter of applying a few disembodied skills. I sometimes work in conjunction with other counsellors, and we temporarily pretend it is possible to separate a person's academic being from their distressed and depressed being. When people are depressed it is essential to take time, and to work at whatever pace is appropriate on that day. This requires knowing how students are feeling, to avoid adding yet further to their sense of pressure and failure. I am always impressed by how well people can look when deep anxiety has taken hold: the heightened colour and upright composure is part of staying alert against what seems to them like imminent disintegration. When people are anxious each word, suggestion and passing comment can be grist to the obsessive mill, leaving students cogitating for days on a throw-away remark which you may not even remember making. Kindness, patience and care are needed to attempt to work at the right pace.

People who are not depressed or particularly anxious can be frightened as well, of writing, of being assessed, of sitting examinations. They are frightened of shadows lurking at the back of the brain: I'll let everyone down, I'm stupid, I'm a fraud, this isn't going to work. Which leads to even heavier thoughts: I'll fail, I have no future, I'll be humiliated, I'll have no life, I'm not worthy of love, or I will not be loved. Talk as much as you like about study, nothing goes in if students' minds are full of sadness and there can be no understanding, comfort or empathy unless you take time at the start of each session to find out how people are feeling. This may well turn out to be the whole session.

How are you feeling?
How are things?
How have you been getting on?
Tell me what's been happening.
Take me through what's been happening.
How are you?
What was the week like?
What's been happening since we last met?
And are you all right?
What's life like at the moment?
Is everything OK?
Last time we met you were quite down. How have things been since then?
What was Christmas/Easter/summer like?
How was the holiday?

Whatever you say always depends on tone of voice: apparently kind phrases can sound accusatory and harsh, and vice versa. The essential elements are to have a genuine interest in the answer and respect for the student's way of life. Sometimes the answers are not nice, and it is scary. People feel suicidal about academic work, but are often too ashamed to admit it. Are you afraid of such feelings in other people? Should you ask questions if you do not really want to know the answers?

I don't know.
It started off all right when I left here, but then it went downhill again.
Well, I gave in the essay.
I had an argument with my tutor.
I've fallen out with my girlfriend.
My friends are fed up with me moaning.
I tried what you'd said and it was useless.
I panicked.

Allow time for people to develop their answers, from tentative statements to honest explanations. It is in silences that we assess how much listeners are actually concerned to hear our accounts of life. Are you able to sit still, without speaking, and convey kindness and interest? Most of us do not know how to speak about academic work, assuming that it just happens, and a listener needs to offer time and patience to help students develop the relevant vocabulary so that they can describe what learning means to them.

Academic history

Understanding how students feel about their work means taking time to explore their personal experiences of education, so that you and they together begin to make sense of the context in which current study problems are happening. Asking about a person's academic history is a waste of time if you merely ask about examination results. Rather, did they enjoy school? If so, what did they enjoy, what did they not enjoy? What did they expect from it, how did school fit into their lives? If it went wrong, when did it begin to go wrong, in what ways? The importance of this kind of discussion is for students to identify their own patterns of responding to being taught. People do not come to university by direct and obvious routes, and the best way to explore this is directly: 'Tell me about coming to university.'

People feel tongue-tied and foolish, for intellectual ability is supposed to mean being able to define, describe, analyse and to come up with the correct solution to problems. To seek help about the one thing you are claiming to be good at, academic work, triggers feelings of humiliation and fraudulence. Of course, for the student concerned, there are a million and one reasons why academic success has not always brought a growth in confidence. For people returning to study after a gap, there is usually an earlier experience of failure and a rooted non-academic identity to be conquered as well. Underneath a range of study problems are a myriad of fears:

I'm going to make a fool of myself.
I'm going to say/do the wrong thing.
I will be judged and found wanting.
My voice is all wrong.
I'm too fat, too thin, I dress badly, . . .
I'm going to do something disastrous.
They will laugh at me.
Everyone else is highly knowledgeable.
Everyone else knows where everything is.
My spelling is poor.
I am too disabled.
I don't think I read properly.
They are nice to me because they feel sorry for me.
Everyone else knows what they are doing.
I am too old.

On arrival, all the other students look happy, relaxed and seem to be walking about purposively. They do not seem to be lost, they are enrolled for all the correct classes, have the right cards, tickets, maps, keys, books, reading lists, and so on. Their local education authorities have come up with the grant cheques, their personal tutors are friendly and approachable. Worse than anything, they all appear to share the same vocabulary, hairstyles, clothes, politics, taste in food, television, music, theatre, books and so forth. You're the one who has no grant, still smokes, eats meat, likes Walt Disney films and has a personal tutor with severe communication problems.

We bring to study the whole of our prior experience. Students coming from school may carry the hopes of their families, the vicarious successes of

parenthood, and whatever hopes they themselves have formed. While research shows us that most students are 'middle-class', this tells a counsellor
or a tutor little about particular students' earlier lives. Family life can be a
source of betrayal, abandonment, cruelty, abuse, and unmeetable conditions – we will love you as long as you pass your examinations, make us
proud, do better than I did, study something useful, stand on your head.
The belief that all 'middle-class' children come straight from standard homes
is naive – individuals also come from institutional care, mental hospitals,
boarding schools, or from the care of relatives. The assumption that no
18-year-old has met death, suicide, illness, accident or pioneering adven-
ture has more to do with adult fantasies about adolescent life than with
reality. And there is no basis for assuming anything about what mature
students may or may not have experienced, for you have no way of knowing
and may never find out. Our capacity to define the undergraduate experience
as 'unreal' leads to unwarranted assumptions about students' past lives,
yet, whatever their age and apparent background, one should never take it
for granted that students have not personally experienced, for example, a
term in prison, cot death, or incest. The disappointments and frustrations
of the first days at university come not just from the inadequacies of the
system, but from what we have expected, and what price has been paid to
get there.

There are, for example, so many reasons for developing 'writer's block'.
One that mature students have come along with regularly over the years is
getting what, to others, seems a reasonable mark for preceding pieces of
work, but being so deeply dissatisfied with the mark that it becomes impossible to do any more written assignments. For some mature students, starting
a degree can mean giving up a home, a job, a business, a house, a car, a
marriage, a family. The need to justify taking up a precious university place
by getting outstanding marks is heightened when the number of 'losses'
experienced is far greater than the 'gains' in merely enrolling for a course.
This kind of audit can only be done when the counsellor/tutor and the
student are feeling quite comfortable with each other:

Profits	*Losses*
possibility of getting a degree	job
reading my favourite subject	money
getting a good qualification	house
possibility of new career	friends in old home
confidence	partner
	children elsewhere
	car
	parents/family
	mobility
	peace of mind
	health/sleep
	confidence

The next piece of assessed work can come to be the focus for all these losses. Unintentionally, to make all this loss worthwhile, people get the idea that only the best marks will do, to justify this level of disruption. A mass of huge life changes have come together, coupled with a sense of bereavement as the past lifestyle disappears, and yet students think they should be grateful and happy because they are at university. Unsurprisingly, the assignment cannot carry the weight of all this justification, and it becomes easier to avoid the task.

The belief that you are not really entitled to a place, or not really clever enough, has a lot of other components apart from justifying major feelings of loss. A sense of being a fraud is commonplace: mature students, in particular, are often aware that they have experienced humiliation and failure in their earlier years of formal education, but are shocked to find how much this still influences academic performance years later. Younger students, too, may have experienced vicious mockery as a standard teaching method, although this will not be obvious from their examination results. Writing, speaking in seminars and any form of assessment can cause panic by providing an opportunity for the institution to 'rumble' the student's stupidity, or so it can seem. Hiding your secret stupidity is in direct conflict with the sang-froid needed to get stuck into these exercises, regardless of whether or not you fall flat on your face. Coupled with an inability to discern what the assessors require of you as a student, a belief in your own stupidity brings back the spectres of past academic failure and childhood terrors.

It can be hard to get people to discuss these elements of academic experience at all (sometimes it is best left until some success brings a little more courage), and words can be too uncomfortable. Drawing pictures of how people see themselves as learners is one starting point with people who have entirely lost their capacity to speak of these matters. Then developing the vocabulary to describe these visual images, moving gently to the point where a description of the image is translated directly into the spoken word without being mediated through crayons or felt-tip pens. A major breakdown in a student's capacity to write or meet assignment deadlines is a temporary withdrawal from academic communication, so it is hardly surprising if speaking about the problems is no more possible than writing academically. Counselling is usually about words, and the absence of words is often what is the problem, so some imagination is required to find nonverbal routes in and around the issues.

It is common for students to miss appointments, and it can be some time, if at all, before you discover why. Occasionally their fear is too great, the risk of changing too overwhelming; sometimes one meeting provides enough reassurance and it is sufficient to know that study problems are fairly common; once in a while a student may have left the university, or just gone home for a break. And in the chaos of backlogs and deadlines, students without diaries just forget appointments. Whatever the cause, I like to write a letter letting people know that they have been missed but without putting them under any pressure to respond or to feel badly about the absence. Writing letters allows one to wish absentees well and is the easiest means of letting people know that they are free to make further appointments should they so wish. A word of warning: if you are writing from a counselling service or from any student support section, be sure not to use 'internal' or used envelopes which refer to you or your service. This breaks confidentiality, and it is surprising how fellow students and staff do pick up these clues.

Starting a degree: expectations and frustrations

Students' prior expectations of undergraduate courses cast long shadows and the first term can bring frustration and disappointment, as well as excitement and new experiences. Without being aware even that they have started out with expectations of university, people experience disappointment and frustration which they find hard to define or pinpoint. A chosen subject can turn out to be entirely different to one's mental picture of it, and subject choice is an expression of identity. Changing subjects is sometimes merely a timetable or timing problem, in which case you need to know the institution well enough so that you can refer on swiftly (if too much time goes by then taking different subjects ceases to be an option). But changing subjects can rock students' daydreams about the future, which are entwined with education. Daydreams are private, personal things, which adults feel shame in sharing, yet they play their part in making disappointment with chosen courses so important.

It is hard to remember how specific people's expectations can be. Old-fashioned notions of Oxford and Cambridge colleges are symbols of British education that represent a system which exists in few places. The notion that you have an individual tutor, for example, with an interest in your intellectual development is still quite common. Small groups, intellectual debate, sherry parties and chamber music playing in the background is a picture far removed from most modern institutions. Universities have, since the 1960s, been places that process large numbers of students in an unusually short period of time from new student to graduate, unlike universities on the mainland of Europe. This full-time system is based on pressure, the lecture system, and individual students taking responsibility for their own study. If this was the case before the 1980s, the recent increases in student numbers have made it even more so, and colleges are now packed to capacity without the necessary increase in staff numbers and resources to match the rise in enrolment figures. While there are many staff working in universities who are concerned to work closely with their students, this is made unlikely by working conditions which ensure that most are overloaded with administration, research, writing and teaching. Wheeler and Birtle (1993: 11) describe how these changes reverberate throughout the whole of an institution, as they discuss and define the role of personal tutors in this pressured system:

On campus teaching space is often cramped and heavily used and classes are large, reducing the personal contact between lecturers and students. Both catering and library facilities tend to be congested, resulting in students having difficulty obtaining basic essentials such as food, course texts, and even in some cases beer.

Lack of close contacts between staff and students results in both groups having limited understanding of the realities of each other's lives, leaving plenty of room for misunderstandings. Unfortunately, those who graduated in the 1960s perpetuate the illusions of punting and picnics, and new students, understandably, feel that their lecturers are deliberately choosing to ignore them for more interesting work. While this might be so for some, the reality for many is that their time is taken up with administration and clerical work. Since the advent of word-processors most now do typing, as well as their own photocopying and filing. While departments are rewarded on the basis of staff publications and books, they do not necessarily provide the requisite facilities, and so staff may well be typing the manuscript of a book in addition to the rest of the clerical work. Students can be unaware that staff absences from the office can be due to employment on part-time or temporary contracts, which are numerous now in universities.

Likewise, staff are not always clear about the impact of low grants on their students' lives. Lack of library books, resources and access to core course material affects how easy or difficult it is to meet deadlines. The pressures involved in just assembling the information for an essay can be great. Poverty precludes the option of buying books when they cannot be easily obtained through a library. The lack of job opportunities after graduation causes fear and apprehension, and lack of casual work in vacations limits earning power and the chances of building up a work history. These concerns influence students' lives to an extent that staff do not always recognize.

If a student is near the beginning of a course it can be helpful for them to write down what they are hoping for out of the course, what their expectations and daydreams are. This account can be embarrassing later, but it is surprising how quickly people forget what it is like to know nothing at all about universities and degree courses. That account gives a point of comparison for later in the year and makes it easier for a tutor/counsellor to ask: 'Are you achieving what you hoped for? Are you living the kind of life you expected?' Surprise can be helpful, disappointment is not always entirely a bad thing. But non-specific frustration which cannot be identified or defined gets in the way like a permanently low cloud. I usually meet people later on, when a course is well under way, and when dissatisfaction is powerful but not understood or located. Here are some areas to explore in study counselling as ways of pinning down and untangling that sense of frustration, irritation or disappointment:

Can you remember what you hoped it would be like when you arrived?
Do you remember why you chose that subject?
And what was it like?

Tell me about the first days at university.
How did you feel at the end of the first term?

Taking time to explore the experience of university can be an eye-opener, for counsellors and for students, who have probably assumed that university is a system into which they must fit. Their own dissident commentary is dismissed as an aberration, a sign of personal failure, rarely welcomed as a relevant or constructive piece in the jigsaw. In spite of daydreams of eccentric dons and creative students, all furiously punting through summer weather, we seem to encourage new students in the belief that 'I' is wrong and has no place in academe.

Who am I talking to?

'Study skills' can present as a means of curing a deficit, giving to students something which they are lacking or correcting whatever it is they are doing wrong. By the time students reach university they are sophisticated learners and this approach alone is not always helpful to their self-confidence, which can filter away in the face of crises. Rather, when confronting a major study challenge, I want students to learn how to marshal their existing knowledge, preferences and experiences to help themselves through. Particularly when all work has ground to a halt, students need the ego-boost of knowing that work recommenced by their own efforts, and not due to the actions of an expert. But making use of your own opinions in the face of apparent failure requires great courage from both mature students and from recent school-leavers, and substantial support, therefore, from a tutor/counsellor.

It is usual to interpret low self-esteem, lack of self-worth and a sense of purposelessness as symptoms of depression, but I also see them as signs of late adolescence in our community. Mature students know that they lack confidence and have been called to account many times to explain their academic interests, by families, partners, children, employers, interviewers and on access courses. Recent school-leavers have rarely experienced that debate in any depth. One regular source of surprise to me is how many people involved in education and universities do not seem to like 18-year-olds. There is the sneer, 'middle-class children'. The commonest cliché is that they are at university because 'it's expected of them', 'to please their parents' and 'to work out what they'll do for a living'. All of these comments may hold some truth, but I am not clear why people who choose to work with recent school-leavers should be so disdainful of them. Younger students pick it up, and devalue their own motivation similarly. If students cannot give you a snappy explanation of their current ambitions and motivation, they, too, will sneer at themselves. In the middle of recession and with high levels of graduate unemployment, undergraduates find it hard to justify and value their activities.

And every generation insists that standards are falling. As well as the national debate about poor spelling, bad punctuation and all the other signs of moral degeneracy, universities have their own list of sins. According to academics over 45, students today do not read as much as they used to, care much more about grades than they should, and are less able to work independently. Set against this background of heckling, getting recent school-leavers to value themselves as learners is not always an easy task:

M: So tell me a bit about yourself.
S: There's nothing to tell really. I went to school, did OK. Then I came here.

Trying to get beyond the blank wall, the assumption that education is some-thing that people do to you, is a slow process. Students feel stupid that they have nothing more to say, so asking questions can be intrusive and merely underline a sense of emptiness. Here are some areas to think about:

Can you remember choosing your current subjects?
Do you know why you chose them?
What seemed appealing about them?
What was unattractive about other subjects?
Did you like school?
Can you say what you liked about school?
Can you say what you didn't like?
What was junior school like?

Sometimes these questions are easily answered, and just act as stepping-stones in the first stages of learning to express preferences and opinions. Often what is said has been in a person's head, but it has never seemed important enough to say, never been of sufficient value to question the implications of an experience. That, of itself, speaks volumes about how little used to expressing their own opinions students can be. We believe that only Victorian children were 'seen but not heard'; in university essays we ask students to state their views with confidence so that we can assess them, straight after years of telling them to 'be quiet'.

Others may wander off the academic route as they talk. Student learning is sometimes discussed as if it floats free from the rest of the world and as if undergraduate life exists in isolation from students' non-academic rela-tionships and prior experiences. Walker (1990: 2) describes how the 'present and the past cannot be seen as existing in purely individual terms', and in the case study of a mature student, 'Suzanne', shows how the wider society, along with Suzanne's mother and grandmother, are intimately interwoven with her depression. You need to be ready for whatever emerges from apparently innocuous questions. Here are some that I have come across:

It was about then that I was raped.
That's when I went into care.
I got arrested for shoplifting.
That was when my mother/sister/brother/father died.
I was getting bullied a lot.

My parents split up about then.
My mother/father remarried.
I went to live with my mother/father.
I missed my brother(s)/sister(s) when we got split up.
It was about then I began to realize I was gay.
My mother/father used to beat me up/sexually abuse me.

The cliché that students are fitting in with their parents' expectations must always have some truth in it. If socialization is effective, then they will share some of their parents' values. However, people will bring their own agenda to their choice of study, although the rest of us may sneer or, on occasion, deny the existence or validity of such agendas. This is not just a British phenomenon. When staying in France, a visiting academic brought his beautiful, youngest daughter to visit for the afternoon. Not surprisingly, she was disgusted with aged English women and lolled around in a state of terminal boredom. But she did spring to life when asked why she had chosen to study law: with animation she described how it fitted into her overall view of life and her commitment to social issues. This animation lasted until her father interrupted her to explain to everyone present that this was all nonsense, she was only doing law to compete with her sister. She sank back into a sullen silence.

Finding what you like, what suits you, and working out your own values is a hard task for most people, whether or not the world permits you to proceed in the direction you would prefer. In some families it is hard for people to hear their own voice, work out what they would like, and they are living out parental and family fantasies to an unpleasant degree. It is not always clear, especially to the participants, what is happening. Where there is a lot of love it can feel like betrayal to go against parents who care so much for you. Yet to parents who just demand what they should do to help their son/daughter complete their backlog of work, my usual answer is that they should 'back off'. I have no illusions about how difficult it is to strike a balance between supportive interest and unhelpful pressure, but parents do need to remember that study is an emotional matter. If, whenever the prospect of studying comes up, a son or a daughter does not mix socially, weeps uncontrollably, throws up whenever they try to work, then the answer is not a new study technique. All these are signs that they do not wish to work. Throwing up regularly over essays is a form of communication. For preference, I see it as healthier to cut out the vomiting and for the student to be able to make a choice and to put that choice into words.

Most adolescents have firm opinions which they have learnt to hide from adults. Mature women students have perhaps spent much of their working life in clerical jobs and as paid or unpaid carers, which have traditionally been roles in which women are encouraged to foster other people's ideas rather than assertively state their own. Personal opinions get buried under all these other social roles. Learning the vocabulary for stating preferences has to be followed by developing the ability to explain these preferences.

Those are the first two steps to forming, stating and communicating your own academic opinions. The first steps do not, immediately, seem to have too much relevance to study:

M: Tell me what sort of things you like doing?

S: What do you mean, like, for fun?

M: (OK, so work is not fun; make a mental note to come back to that.) Well, whatever, what comes to mind.

S: I like football.

M: What do you enjoy about football?

S: I like playing, just kicking a ball about, no reason really. Kills time.

M: Mm?

S: Well, you forget all this stuff, just join in, play with the lads, it's not important, you just do it. You don't have to make a thing out of it. Do you know what I mean?

M: I'm not sure what 'making a thing out of it' means.

S: Well, you don't have to write about it, revise, you don't get tested on it. If I do badly, it doesn't matter, my future doesn't hang in the balance, you don't have the parents on your back. You just do it.

M: What have you been doing this week?

S: Nothing much. Just watched telly.

M: What have you watched?

S: *EastEnders, Neighbours, Home and Away.*

M: What were they like this week?

S: All right. I don't rate *Neighbours* much at the moment, I've gone off it a bit.

M: Why's that?

S: Oh I don't know, it's all so stupid. I just feel I'm wasting time when I watch it.

M: Mm?

S: Well, it's all indoors. At least with *Home and Away* it feels younger, they go out and do things. With *Neighbours* it's all inside their houses, it reminds me of being at home with nothing to do.

S: I'm supposed to write a crit of this play, I can't do it.

M: OK, do you know why not?

S: I dunno, I can't think of anything to say.

M: Let's start with you describing the play to me.

S: Yeah. It's about this man, and he has a crisis, and they all shout at each other, and then it gets left up in the air. (Silence.) That's about it, really. (Silence.)

M: Does his crisis make any sense to you?

S: No. It's all stupid. It's supposed to be some kind of searing social commentary, but it's a waste of paper really.

M: So what's his crisis supposed to be about?

S: Well, he goes to work one day in this insurance office. It's set in London, in the City. He gets the same train every day with the same people, they're all commuters. He goes to this huge open-plan office, and they spend all day going through insurance claims. It's about turning your back on materialism, apparently.

M: And how does he do it?

S: Well, it starts off with him being subversive, like fiddling with bits and pieces of forms. Then he starts on the computers, and changing the money, the figures. So, like, is he making a stand or just being a thief?

M: So this play, is it set on one day, or over time, or what?

S: No, it's all about this one day when he goes in and is questioned by these investigators, who are supposed to be some kind of metaphor for conscience and state, at least that's what someone said in a seminar.

M: And what do you say?

S: I dunno. I just took them as real people.

M: And do they seem like real people?

S: Well no, that's part of the problem. They're, like, cardboard. You'd never meet them on the train.

The initial stages are about highly personal likes and dislikes, using whatever material is to hand from students' lives. Becoming used to just speaking aloud and being found interesting can be a major step forward. Valuing 'I' as relevant to the academic process, recognizing one's experience as integral to learning. Only then is it possible to start translating personal preferences into academic language. This is a quite open and self-conscious intent to 'translate' into another language, and a lot of time is saved by being honest about doing this intentionally. This is rarely the moment to become embroiled in debates about the reality of truth and language, that can come later when fluency is more confidently established.

Personal experience and one's sense of self can, on occasion, be central to why progress cannot be made. So, for example, it is not unknown for mature students to find essays analysing the postwar education system impossible to complete. That personal story needs examination, sometimes even 'writing out' clears one's mind as well as acknowledging the importance of experience. The next step is to look at why that personal tale is hard to translate into the academic form – what elements in both the story and the form resist expression?

Aims when talking

For people who expect all study work to be snappy and directive, the sorts of conversations described in this chapter will seem woolly and directionless.

However, the starting point to improving how students work is to examine what they do already, so that they can develop their personal style. The main aim is to foster in students sufficient confidence for them to adjust and adopt new study techniques to suit an existing way of working, which is usually more successful than suggesting methods by which one becomes a different person. To achieve this means spending a lot of time discovering and examining academic preferences as well as committing large amounts of time to thinking about how these fit into the student's overall life.

These aims engage a tutor/counsellor in far more questioning than might be the case in counselling relationships. Asking questions is always a risky business, which is invasive and can be hurtful. Questions should develop from what students say, as ways of helping unravel their thoughts, rather than as a diagnostic tool by which one ticks off items from the expert tutor's predecided agenda. Jacobs (1988) describes basic techniques which are common to many forms of counselling, amongst which are 'exploratory responses' (1988: 31–2) and 'information-seeking responses' (1988: 32–3). In addition to the well-known techniques of listening, observation and reflecting responses, these two other responses are, in fact, questions. Among professionals questioning usually indicates who is taking the lead and who is in control, but by viewing questions as 'responses', one is reminded that questioning can be used differently from this 'control' model when working co-operatively with fellow adults. As Jacobs describes, an exploratory response is a means of drawing out something which may be hinted at in non-verbal ways, but is not necessarily obvious to the client; information-seeking responses are, as implied, used for clarification and always run the risk of being 'closed' questions (see Jacobs 1988: 19–39). Open questions are ones which allow people to develop their thoughts, and can rarely be answered quickly or succinctly, such as: 'How did you feel about the mark you got for that essay?' Closed questions may be necessary to form a picture of exactly what a student's work situation looks like, how much work is left to be done, and what immediate, formal, conditions are being laid down by departments. Open questions are usually the ones which help in working towards the aim of helping students develop their own styles of study and to find personal strategies for overcoming the challenges they face. It is quite hard to move from closed to open questions, and closed questions can abruptly shut down a more open, exploratory conversation.

A part of 'reflective' responses is summarizing what has been said. This might be to help when students have become stuck or lost their way. It can be a useful precursor to finishing a session, to check out that you have properly understood what a student has been trying to say, and combined with the question 'Is that a fair summary?' gives the student a sense of having talked in a coherent way. Care should always be taken not to summarize in a manner reminiscent of a judge's summing up; phrases like 'you said' can easily sound doubting and accusatory. 'Is that a fair summary?' is a useful question if students correct you – perhaps the words are right but the tutor/counsellor is emphasizing the wrong aspects or missing out relevant matters. Finishing on an integrated note (where appropriate) helps you to understand students' priorities better.

Longer-term goals can get buried if working with one student for some period of time as day-to-day academic crises take precedence. The technique of 'reviewing' can be helpful both to students and tutor/counsellors – for example, reviewing progress:

> When we first met you were very concerned about taking notes from reading, how does that seem now?
> A few weeks ago you weren't sleeping or eating much. I get the impression you've moved on quite a bit. How does it feel from where you are?

It may feel quite different to the student, which is important for you to acknowledge and to think about. If your impression of a person's life is quite different to their own view, one must ask how carefully you have been attending to them. It may be that by reviewing progress a wider set of issues surfaces: a student's difficulty with self-congratulation, or fear in the face of success. Reviewing progress is not about judging whether or not a student's performance has improved, but whether or not what you are doing together is experienced as helpful or appropriate. People's work ambitions change as they begin to grow in confidence, and these changing aims on the part of the student need to be made central to the process, rather than just working away at an out-of-date agenda.

> We said when we first met that we would meet three times to think about reading and writing, and then see how things seemed. How does it all look to you now?
> You've cleared a large backlog of work this term. How would you like us to proceed from here?
> How would you like to use these sessions next term?

This last question, of course, can only be asked when it is obvious the student wishes to meet you again. It should be clear in the relationship that the student always holds the option to call a halt to meeting a tutor/counsellor.

Working in universities, unlike other counselling settings, means that relationships with students are broken up into chunks of time called 'terms'. These provide an ideal opportunity to help students look backwards and forwards over their academic experience, and work out what suits them and what they wish to work towards. It can be useful for students to take ten minutes per term to review their academic situation, and tutor/counsellors can help by taking time to ask: 'What did you like, what did you not like? What suits you, and what is causing you difficulty?' It is not always possible to change what students do not like, but energy can be focused on what needs improving.

From this process, students learn that their own preferences are of central importance, and this includes assessing work according to their own standards, not just those of tutors. Undergraduates are expected to take responsibility for their own work, so students need to learn to review work according to their own standards and values, not just according to the marks others give them or what parents, friends or colleagues approve. 'Reviewing' is a positive process: rather than students berating themselves for being, for example, not able to work to deadlines, the knack is to take five minutes to imagine constructive ways of improving and to pinpoint the areas they would like to develop.

Reviewing is positive because it allows students to revise their expectations in the light of experience, and this revision is the start of a journey out of frustration and disappointment. Once caught up in deadlines and course demands, it can be hard for students to remember what their hazy, personal ambitions might have been. It can, on occasions, lead to the decision to quit a course, or it might lead to changing courses. It can result in valuing those aspects of a course which are satisfying and achieving a better understanding of why other parts do not satisfy, hence a greater self-knowledge. Revising personal aims is rewarding only once students realize that meeting institutional demands does not have to equal abandoning their personal experience and vantage point for ever. Differing personal aims affect how courses are approached, while course tutors might have entirely different sets of aims again for their students. Reading, particularly, is an activity which varies considerably according to the purpose in reading a text, and in the next chapter we examine ways of proceeding when students have become stuck with this activity which is so central to academic work.

5

Stuck 1: Reading

Academic reading provides the information and material which forms much of the content of students' writing assignments, by which they are assessed. Hence, there is a double pressure for students when reading: to understand the material and to reach an acceptable standard in coursework or examinations. The traditional advice offered is: read the assignment title, analyse it, read, collate notes, write a plan and then write up the final, edited version, whether it be essay, project work or laboratory reports. When I meet students they might have been stuck on work for some time, and reiterating the traditional formula for completing assignments is rarely helpful.

My own hopes are that at the end of our meetings students can begin to develop strategies to: return to reading with an improved capacity to control panic; confront decisions about selection of reading matter; learn to gain an overall sense of a text; involve themselves with complex detail, obscure vocabulary and difficult language use; cope reasonably with practical matters such as using the library; and approach reading with a critical mind, while getting some fun out of the whole process. I always have to ensure that I am listening carefully when people talk about reading, because as a student I found myself powerfully silenced by academic texts. While I read ferocious amounts, I approached each piece as if it were fiction, extracting the overall plot for private consumption but never daring to engage in debate with writers in the semi-public manner demanded by written assignments and examinations. So for my practice it is especially important that I do not produce a curriculum which would have met my undergraduate needs rather than those of the student expressing concerns. Reading and writing are central to the work of professional academics, and tutor/ counsellors as well as students have to take care not to get bogged down in expert opinion and forget to put the individual student's needs at the centre of the process. A simple way of ensuring this is regularly to check out the student's experiences of reading, by discussing their responses, preferences and problems with academic reading.

Working with highly able adults means that while one minute they may be unusually sophisticated in thinking and knowledge, the next minute may reveal a lack of awareness of basic elements, and to help students to progress requires sufficient responsiveness to move quickly between these different levels of knowledge. Learning how to read and write academically when you have become entirely stuck requires some stripping away of assumptions and working habits, and involves going back to check understanding of basic tasks. However it is achieved, undergraduates have to learn to be selective in their reading: not only is it impossible for them to read every text on a reading list, but also they need to know how to select relevant extracts from within a text. This process requires confidence in one's judgement, as well as developing the skills of skimming or skip-reading and summarizing. Selection, most of all, requires of students that they engage with the content of a text in order to make judgements about its relevance and meanings, rather than just aiming for speedy coverage of quantities of material.

General problems with reading

A superficial analysis would say that reading is merely the business of decoding symbols, while fluency is about decoding quantities of symbols at speed and accurately. It is nothing as simple as that, however, and Donaldson (1978) has argued that, unlike the spoken word which can appear to be a continuous sound, the written word breaks up the message, and does so without the accompanying cues of gesture and physical environment. So in learning to read we also learn to reflect on the tools of communication as well as the message: perception of form as well as content goes hand-in-hand with awareness of one's own thinking and the seeds of intellectual self-control. Hence, the choices novice readers learn to make about meanings are, in Donaldson's (1978: 95) thesis, the basis 'for the development of the kinds of thinking which are characteristic of logic, mathematics and the sciences' (see Donaldson 1978: 86–95).

Certainly, as Donaldson's thesis implies, each stage of learning needs to do more than just meet performance requirements at a given moment in time. The skills needed to tackle the next set of intellectual demands must also be sown. Reading continues to be a constant search for meanings coupled with reflection upon and analysis of words and language use. Usually the concern for older children is to encourage them to read fiction for pleasure, with the assumption that the criteria for judging a 'good reader' are: reading the whole of a text from the first to the last page, in that order, and reading from left to right with a consciousness of the worth of each word, albeit speedily covered. I suspect that as children learn to read quickly and flawlessly, then overt analysis of language becomes a specialist activity only, carried out only by students of literature and language. Once children have overcome the hurdle of learning to read sufficiently well, aloud, for their age group, reading does not appear to be addressed as problematic. Yet reading tasks continue to change as people go through different stages in their education and as they face varied academic tasks, and undergraduates need to be able to reflect upon language use as they read. Säljö

(1984: 73) describes how reading at university is a summary of centuries of debate, and is usually complex and abstract: 'Reading . . . is a strategy for taking part in ways of conceptualizing the world that are frequently abstract and unrelated to everyday experiences in any obvious way.' The commonest style of writing met at university is unlikely to be descriptive of the world around us, and is, hence, abstract, and factual information, whether scientific or otherwise, will be grounded in the years of intellectual debate and modes of thinking which have gone before. The fixed belief that students should understand a text at one sitting, in a similar manner to reading a novel, is one of the biggest barriers to academic progress.

A limited view of what reading is about can encourage unwary students into difficulties with work. The inflexibility with which a concept of reading is held hinders progress: so a study counsellor may not be believed or trusted when explaining a variety of approaches to reading if a student holds the fixed belief that they should read the whole of every text. When this is coupled with the expectation that a 'good reader' grasps the meaning of a text instantly, as when reading, for example, a novel for pleasure, then a student's energy can be put into covering up panic triggered by not understanding the text. Reading is so central to the idea of a degree that people are, understandably, reluctant to acknowledge this area of panic to an outsider.

Assuming that all students share academics' love of the written and printed word is naive. There are students who loathe reading and others who are on the wrong courses. Occasionally one meets students who have had their reading predigested by teachers and that digest given as handouts, or have even had the page numbers picked out in advance for them to read. This means that while qualified, students may not have learned the skills needed to tackle degree-level work or to consider how the process of selection when reading might, of itself, contribute to their overall understanding and knowledge. Nor have they learnt the vital lesson that there are different styles of reading according to the text and one's purpose in reading it.

Exercise 5.1 helps ensure that students, no matter how experienced as readers, cover these basic elements. It introduces the notion that reading is an activity to question and about which they do know something. One introduction to asking these kinds of question is to imagine having to explain academic reading to a new student.

Exercise 5.1: Reading for a degree

1. What reasons are there for reading at university?
2. As children we are taught to read all words, and the whole of every text. But there are other ways of reading which adults use every day – describe some of these other styles of reading.
3. How would you describe an 'academic' style of reading?
4. What skills do students need to read effectively?

A common response to academic reading is one of dread, along with the expectation that the work will be too difficult to understand. This is about self-image: the belief that you are so stupid that any erudite or informed piece of writing is bound to be incomprehensible to you. Whatever brings that attitude into being, it means the first study task is to turn the text into accessible, comprehensible lumps. This is probably different to tutors' hopes, which are more likely to be about wanting students to engage with the text at a critical, analytical level. Consequently students' secret assessments of how long it will take to read a piece will usually vary substantially from the tutor's assessment, even though publicly students may guess a time somewhat nearer the tutor's estimate. Individuals will assume that their fellow students take the shorter amount of time to read.

Reading provides a rich body of information about what constitutes academic writing in a chosen discipline. Academic writing, for example, rarely demands characterization in the way good fiction might, even though social science interview material can give a strong sense of how people feel about life. Nor does academic writing generally ask readers to develop an empathic sense of place through descriptive prose of the kind which might be found in travel books. Most undergraduates are unaware that they already know these facts about academic style, and as a helper you need to provide stepping-stones which allow people insight into what they know already about academic reading and writing, before moving on to add new knowledge and insights. Many students have learnt the expression 'speed reading' and believe that techniques taught to speed up their coverage of material will cure a backlog, whereas it will often intensify the problems. What is needed is the ability to engage with meanings in difficult, abstract texts, to read in different ways according to the particular purposes in reading, and gather sufficient confidence to locate and select relevant material.

Emergency measures

Students may have stopped reading altogether by the time I meet them, and this needs to be addressed before moving on to the more complex and interesting issues surrounding reading. Symbolically, students stagger into a counselling room under the dead weight of bags full with library books, occasionally strapped to their backs in haversacks like a terrible Greek punishment. This package of work which must be done is carried everywhere, in the vain hope that today will be different to yesterday. At this stage there is just sickening anxiety and no ability to concentrate on the printed word, which has become a trigger for panic. No amount of debate about critical reading or the joys of education will help until this initial block is overcome. The unattractiveness of academic language is of even greater importance than usual, and one word of jargon can be enough to trigger avoidance.

I find it useful to work through a book with students when they have reached this lowest point, which is the academic equivalent of holding someone's hand, to give a bit of courage and support while facing the feared object, in this case an academic textbook. By working together to get an overall idea of what a book is about, students develop a simple framework by which to understand a text quite rapidly, and the speed of this exercise comes as an immense relief. Explaining a text to a stranger also stops one's mind wandering off to the remaining pile of work waiting to be done, so encourages some focused concentration and rehearses, in a safe setting, some 'good reading' practices.

First, students choose which text or part of text has to be read. This may mean referring to an essay title or seminar topic, which acts as a signpost indicating the kinds of material to be selected. This is followed by checking contents pages, the indexes at the back of books and some of the headings within chapters. The next step is to get an overall 'feel' of a piece which the student has decided should be read in depth. Before starting to read the whole piece, they need to find out what the text is about: the title, the introductions and the headings or subtitles should provide a lot of information about the message of the text. The more a reader has worked out before starting to read (in the more traditional sense of the word), the easier it becomes to interpret complex arguments and difficult vocabulary. 'Summary sheets' are a useful aid to writing a synopsis or description of the text before getting involved in detailed reading. A summary sheet (see the example below) is a piece of paper on which the student records the full reference, a synopsis and any further details selected as important. The synopsis may be a description of the text, or a résumé of the author's intentions, and is most helpful if filled in *before* reading a text in detail. Details can be recorded after reading the text or, if students can trust themselves to be scrupulously selec-

---

Summary Sheet

Reference:

'The Common Toad', pp. 30–38, Ch. 5, in *Reptiles and Habitats*, C.C. Jones (ed.), London: Bollinger. (Library reference: XXXXYYY.67.)

Summary:

Other details:

---

tive, during reading. This approach is useful where access to a text is for a very limited amount of time, as it helps focus the mind on being selective.

Not all writing styles lend themselves easily to this exercise, and oblige students to struggle much more to produce a synopsis. A philosophical argument might wend its way through a whole book in a manner much more akin to fiction than will be the case with standard textbooks. Students should be encouraged to make a note of these responses to writing styles and consider (when there is time) what the style is telling readers about the author's intentions and assumptions. If reading novels or plays, students can write a brief synopsis for each chapter or scene and note which characters appear in that segment, while considering what their presence contributes to that part of the work.

Flick through to see how long the chosen text is, so that the reader does not dive in at the beginning and attempt to plough through, with no sense of how much there is to read. To visualize the structure of a piece of reading, students can decide how much of it is introductory, explanatory or concluding, so that they are always aware of being in a 'section'. Reading sections adds up to reading a whole piece, without attempting to blunder through from beginning to end, especially with a reluctant reader. It is easier to resume work if interrupted in a section, rather than rereading a whole piece, and small chunks can be summarized more readily.

Asking questions: personal and academic

This reintroduction to reading is intended to build confidence and kick-start the academic process, and is not a recipe which students should stick to as the correct reading method. Once they are under way again, and not faced with crushing deadlines and anxiety, then approaches to reading can be developed along much more personal lines. This personal approach must be relevant to their subjects as well as taking into account individual preferences and the critical requirements of scholars in their disciplines. Stepping-stones are provided by exploring reading in general and one's personal preferences:

   Do you like reading?
   How do you feel about reading?
   What do you read for pleasure?
   What kind of reading helps you to relax?
   What does reading do for you personally?

These questions are invasive and personal. In a university, where it is assumed that the written word is central to knowledge, life and the 'acceptable' person, admitting that you do not like to read requires trust. My aim is to encourage students to develop confidence in what they do and to graduate with an awareness of their own academic interests, as the basis for a lifetime's growth, and not to teach my particular academic values. If you are reading women's studies, admitting that you only enjoy romantic novels or comics requires a sense of safety and a certainty of confidentiality. Hence a counsellor requires sensitivity in the manner of asking questions and in knowing when to broach these questions.

Reading at university *is* difficult, and probably the last time students, of whatever age, met any real barriers to reading would have been as children struggling at home or at primary school. One should always be alert to how reading has been the precursor to public humiliation for many children and, among mature students especially, a prelude to violent punishment in childhood. Martin (1989) has written of how children who struggle with reading can perceive teaching quite differently to the teacher's good intentions: so, while the teacher allows more time to hear a struggling child read aloud, the child's anxiety levels go up as they feel more tested and checked-up on. Reading aloud, then, the only way a teacher can find out what is happening, becomes a source of added stress. Childlike embarrassment can be stirred up in adults, especially if they did have specific problems with reading. Where the teacher's intention was not helpful but was to humiliate the child, for example, by laughing at them in front of the class then working with another person on the process of reading can be excruciating torture for adults. Why well-qualified people dislike reading is worthy of close examination, but a study counsellor needs to be alert to when this is too painful a subject for students to explore in depth.

Questioning is a technique students can use to develop awareness of how academic reading informs us about different purposes in writing. By viewing academic writing as one medium for written communication among many one can start to question how writing intentions shape styles of writing. A fun introduction to this area is to find a variety of newspaper articles on the same story and analyse the differences in style. Who are they talking to? Make a list of the facts of the story, drawn from every article, then go back and see how many facts each article uses, how they are used and if particular facts get used more than others. Even when students are highly sophisticated readers, this understanding of writing can get buried when anxiety has taken a hold for some time.

Another version of the same exercise is shown below as Exercise 5.2, and can be worked through with groups as well as individual students.

Exercise 5.2: Newspaper stories

Take an essay/project title. Explain what you would have to do to produce your usual written assignment; now imagine having to write a newspaper article – what would you do with that material?

Exercise 5.2 does not ask people to write both pieces of work, just to explain clearly what issues are involved in producing the finished work; what constrains writers in both media and what releases them? Tutors and counsellors would be prompting with such questions as what language and sentence construction are permitted by each medium, and how you use information in each medium.

One other important question for students to ask when reading is: 'What constitutes "data" in my chosen subjects?' 'Data' is a word which covers a variety of types of knowledge: in many subjects data is 'scholastic', based on a thorough understanding of the published writings and arguments of others. What is confusing for students is that, in one sense, all their work is made up of this kind of scholasticism – that is how they master the rudiments of a discipline – yet they may well be studying a subject which, in fact, values empirical, primary research. So, when reading in this scholastic manner, students could be learning to compare the quality of authors' experiments, surveys, interviews, documentary evidence or analysis and textual analysis. Students find it hard to know what it means when they are told to 'put some of yourself' into academic writing as assignments appear to test their capacity to review other people's work.

Moving on

The study counsellor's first aim is to get students back to opening books, and preliminary work is intended to help students take back some control over their work. This does not address the problem of academic language: for those not fully socialized into their subjects of study, academic language appears unnecessarily cumbersome and exclusive. When reading fiction there is a tacit expectation that the writer will work to include the reader, to communicate a message. Academic writing is not experienced as similarly communicative, and what is judged to be essential, albeit specialist, vocabulary can be seen by the reader as jargon – that is, as unhelpfully obtuse and exclusive language.

It may take a lot of work to help a student to move beyond getting a general grasp of a text once a crisis has passed, and to dare, instead, to

---

Exercise 5.3: Words

Keep a list of specialist words in a separate notebook. Use the back of the book for the list. Add to the list (not in alphabetical order) as you come across specialist words, phrases or jargon that you do not understand. From time to time, spend ten minutes in the library looking up one word or phrase in specialist glossaries or dictionaries, and only do one at a time. Later in the day, when away from the library, write down your understanding of the word or phrase, and put that at the front of your book in whatever order you choose.

Also write down any thoughts or feelings you have about the word, its uses, its meanings, and any similar words which might do the same job. Are these synonyms, in fact, *exactly* the same or do they miss or add some nuance of meaning? So, at the front of your book, you deal with the word or phrase under three headings:

  (i) meaning;
 (ii) your thoughts and feelings about it;
(iii) and a comment on any likely synonyms.

---

grapple with detail. Not understanding the details of a piece of reading sparks off feelings of anxiety, and students can start to avoid reading again as they fear a return of the original crisis. Exercise 5.3 is one way of helping students come to terms with complex language, and to bring into the open the fear of their own responses to jargon and specialist vocabulary. In the early stages of this kind of work I occasionally suggest people jot down a list of specialist words and bring those to our next meeting, if this feels comfortable. It may be that a pattern of avoidance is being set up under the guise of 'I don't have time to do all that stuff', and together we can begin to examine a person's responses to words and meanings.

A common experience among readers is to get bogged down in detail, and to reread the same section many times, without improving understanding. Instead of letting people continue to blame themselves when this happens, one route away from the problem is to reflect back on the text for 'jars' that are impeding understanding. Some questions students can ask are:

• Is the author's style clear?
• Do they use long, imprecise or unnecessary words?
• Is their vocabulary unnecessarily difficult?
• Is the author's development of argument or thought confused?
• Has the author wandered from their own main point or argument?

This gives panicky students a clear course of action, although it is not a foolproof method as the problems are not always easy to trace.

An important reading decision which students learn to take is when to involve themselves with detail and when to work on overall meanings of a text. To do this, they need to develop flexibility in reading styles. Unlike reading for pleasure, different purposes in reading require different approaches to texts. One way to explore these issues is to ask what it is possible for one person to read in the course of a day. A list might look like this:

newspapers	TV schedules
advertisements	cooking instructions/packets of food
textbooks	patterns
sides of buses	job advertisements
bills	leaflets
recipes	posters
manuals – computer/cars/machinery	novels
labels	letters
signposts	record sleeves
pamphlets	competition rules
magazines	tickets
timetables	price tags/sizes

If someone really cannot get their head round the task, an alternative question to ask is where you come across printed and written words during the day.

The next area to explore is how we go about reading these different materials. A gentle introduction is to select two dissimilar modes of reading (such as bus timetable and novel), and to work out how both you and the student go about reading. Hopefully, you will find different approaches according to the purpose in reading, and personal differences between both of you. So, when people are relaxed enough to admit to it, you find that some readers prefer to read novels only if they have read the last few pages first. Words and phrases that come up regularly are: browsing, skipping, selecting, daydreaming, finding the right bit, reading from beginning to end. It is possible that a student already practises these different types of reading, but does so secretively. The belief that one must read every book on a reading list and from cover to cover dies hard. Students can take a lot of convincing that scanning a text, selecting relevant extracts and skipping the inessentials is the core approach to much academic reading. They see this as cheating and cutting corners.

The important question to draw out is: 'Why am I reading this?' Active reading is required, that is, asking specific questions, whether you are looking for particular information or asking a more general question such as what the author's central argument is or what the end of the story is. I use the following questions for students to work out how to approach reading with a few simple questions in mind. In one-to-one meetings it will take as long as the particular student needs it to take, and can either be set out formally on a handout for people to work with privately or asked directly, in a shortened and friendlier form, if there is sufficient trust not to cause the student any embarrassment.

1. We read different books, chapters and articles for different purposes, and those purposes affect the style of reading required. What different purposes can you think of, and what approaches to reading do these purposes demand?
2. Active reading means engaging with the text, rather than letting words swim passively in front of your eyes. We do this by actively analysing the structure, style and content of a passage. What basic questions can you ask about a text before reading it?

Taking notes and using libraries

What notes students take depends on their purpose in reading, which dictates the selection of information according to the task in hand. Essay titles, seminar titles, and project titles indicate the sorts of material needed from reading. Students who have become highly anxious find it almost impossible to decide on what to select, being afraid of missing out something vital. It requires confidence or desperation to make these choices, and occasionally students do not produce essays because they have become caught in an endless round of transcribing 'notes' from reading, but are actually copying out chunks of books. Some kind staff indicate chapters and passages to be read, but ultimately this delays the agony involved in making independent decisions about selection of relevant material. These selection decisions are the first, essential step to writing essays, projects, laboratory reports and any other form of academic writing.

Selection decisions are not easy to make, not least because the subject matter is rarely clear-cut. Not all topics have final, complete answers, there can be ambiguity, dissension and contradictory material, and these complexities are not always sanitized for undergraduates in the way that earlier teaching may have done. Exercise 5.4 is made up of the most basic questions about note-taking, which can be discussed gently in one-to-one meetings. My experience of using these questions is that most people know the theory of note-taking, but are not prepared either to go into details or to match the theory to what they actually do. Most commonly, students take notes because they are afraid of missing out something important and rarely because they see the noted information as useful to them. So these areas need to be explored, not merely glibly glossed over.

Exercise 5.4: Note-taking

• Why take notes when reading?
• When should you take notes from reading?
• What kind of information might you want to note when reading?

Students do assume that if they struggle with a text this is because they are stupid. Exercise 5.5 is designed to short-circuit this by making the assumption that there are elements in the text which affect the ease or otherwise of note-taking. Learning to recognize the ways in which a text triggers panic is one of the bridges between grasping general meanings and learning to involve oneself in detailed language and data. It is helpful if done as part of an academic course, if a simple, short, text relevant to the subject is provided.

Exercise 5.5: Difficulty with note-taking

General:

• What makes it difficult to take notes?
• What helps you to take notes?

Specific:

• What is there about this piece of writing which makes it difficult to take notes?
• What is there about this piece of writing which helps you to take notes?

In individual sessions this can be worked through, without doing the actual note-taking, while using a text the student has to work on.

Learning to research one's own material reaches beyond gaining sufficient confidence to read academic material and taking notes efficiently, it means using available resources more effectively. Students need to make a friend of the university library at the earliest possible opportunity. As well as going on any tours available (and going on them as often as possible), it helps occasionally just to wander round and get the 'feel' of a library. Even if students find it hard to work for long periods in libraries, time can be usefully spent occasionally browsing through newspapers, journals and books. The more at home people are in libraries, the easier it becomes to make full use of them. Students are not necessarily expected to know everything about their subjects, but they are usually expected to be skilled at tracking down relevant information when it is needed. Making full use of the library means developing the ability to track down information, to carry out research, without being told where information is, to start to explore a topic without knowing whether or not appropriate information exists, but to find it if it does.

However, once a course gets under way, it becomes too easy just to race in to the library, grab any books that are on the list, and race off again. Few universities have sufficient course texts for the numbers of students looking for them. Popular course books are often used for only a few weeks in the year, but unfortunately during those few weeks most students on a given course want the same books so that they can write the same essays. Libraries try to get round this by running some variation of a 'short loan' system, whereby a book can be borrowed for a severely limited period of time, enforced with heavy fines. Reference libraries, from which books cannot be removed but where students can work, are also an option, as long as there is sufficient space for increased numbers of students to work. The alternative is to spend the library's annual budget on multiple copies of one book only.

All libraries run introductory tours for new students and, usually, go to great lengths to make themselves accessible to students. But if a student is feeling fraudulent and stupid, a university library is still a daunting place no matter how helpful staff try to be. For those who are not feeling phobic about their library, students can take themselves on personal conducted tours, and make better sense of how libraries work by having a series of questions to help them. Having questions to answer gives a sense of purpose, rather than the embarrassment of aimless wandering. It is most helpful if you help students to draw up lists of questions relevant to their own courses, but, failing that, some simple suggestions which can be made are:

What is the system used to catalogue books?
Where do I find social science books? Arts, science, law, where are
    they kept?
Where are the journals kept?
How long can books be borrowed for, does this vary according to the
    book?
Can I reserve books?
Are there special 'work' areas for students?

What is the system for recalling books?
What coins/cards do I need to photocopy in the library?
What is microfiche? What would I find recorded on it?
I know the name of an author – how can I find out the title of the book?
I know the name of a book, how can I find it?
The book I want is not on the shelf – how can I find out where it is?

Critical reading

Reading academic material is not just about becoming an elegant reader who can grasp the overall sense of a piece, translate jargon in order to extract facts from a text, while taking notes efficiently. Ideally, readers should learn to engage with a text in a way which enables them to assess its worth. This is not, as many believe, about being cynical or slating all academic work for the sake of it. Being critical does not mean being permanently negative, sarcastic, or down-putting of all other opinion, nor is it quibbling about anything which is said or taught. Rather, being critical is learning to assess the logic and rationale of arguments and the quality of the substantiating data. Instead of flaw-hunting, it is being able to ask how important the flaws are, and so to weigh the worth of evidence. This means being able to ask questions of the text beyond what it means, what it is saying.

Asking people to come up with their own questions to ask of a text can be so far outside students' current understanding of what is involved in academic work that it can be counter-productive to pursue too directly at first. Your role as a helper is to be sufficiently sensitive to know when a line of work adds to a student's sense of failure and stupidity. Rather than pushing people uncomfortably fast, you can work on a text together. If the student provides a chapter or short piece which they need to read, then you can provide a few simple questions to help give them a flavour of how to approach reading critically. There are a variety of simple questions one can start with, and these are just a few suggestions for the early stages of developing students' critical faculties:

1. What are the authors' intentions in writing this piece?
2. When reading the introductory paragraph, ask yourself what kinds of information and argument might be expected to follow in the main body of the text.
3. What issues do the authors see as important, given the questions they have chosen to address?
4. What other questions might they have asked, and why do you think they did not?

Working together means, in this case, helping a student to piece together answers to these questions with your help and support. It asks the student to explain a lot about the piece to you, and practises using a text, rather than reading it like a story. You both go backwards and forwards through the pages, searching for answers, selecting out relevant bits of information, all within a framework of an overall 'feel' of what the piece is about. The first steps, before asking evaluative questions, have been to translate the piece, to make sure the student understands what it is about and what the author's specific argument is.

> *M:* OK. What you've said so far is this: the book is about the distribu-
> tion of toads in Cumbria. The author's argument seems to be that
> to understand why they are found in such odd concentrations you
> need to know something about genetic mutation as well as about
> land use and climate. Is that about right?
>
> *S:* Yeah.
>
> *M:* Does it make sense?
>
> *S:* Sort of, I mean yes, I can work out what they're saying now ...
>
> *M:* But?
>
> *S:* Well, it doesn't fit with what was said in the lecture, she said they'd
> only studied toads in Cumbria for two years, no one had done it
> before.
>
> *M:* I don't understand.
>
> *S:* Well, that's not a lot of time to draw conclusions about genetic
> mutations, is it?
>
> *M:* So you're not sure how safe the evidence is?

A conversation like this would go on to discuss: what was said in the relevant lectures; how and why this differs from what has been read; and what clashes of information like this can imply. I would want the student to understand how vital a point like this is to unravelling questions about research, the worth of information and alternative viewpoints. Undergraduates usually think a topic does not make sense because they are stupid instead of accepting their own confusion as a reasonable response.

As Säljö (1984) has indicated, academic reading is much more than covering relevant facts. As the means by which a student enters a conceptual world which is grounded in many years of debate, it is also the route by which one learns what the currency of research is in a given discipline, that is, what constitutes data. The language use, the vocabulary, the styles of writing, the ways of drawing conclusions, the aims of academic endeavour are all embedded in any set piece of reading and need to be decoded as much as the piece needs to be translated into comprehensible English. 'Not understanding' can be as much about a growing awareness of one's exclusion from some dimly sensed discourse as it can be about not comprehending the actual words in a text. In effect, students are breaking in on a private debate between current practitioners of a discipline as well as between past and present ones, and frequently admit to being uncomfortable among the 'giants' of their chosen courses of study. Students may love their subjects, but one lesson learnt soon after arrival at university is that the subjects belong to other, powerful, competitive, people, as Becher (1981: 109) has written: 'Disciplines are also cultural phenomena: they are embodied in collections of like-minded people, each with their own codes of conduct, sets of values and distinctive intellectual tasks.'

For many students all of this is of little consequence, they are happy just to get back to reading and meeting deadlines. Others do worry and cannot relax until they make more sense of what is implicit in a text as well as what is explicit. Some experience the exclusiveness of the subject they have loved for years as frustrating and distressing.

For those who chose a course out of interest, with the hopes of exploring it in more depth, doing a degree in one's favoured subject can lead to immense frustration. Interest and enjoyment of reading can get buried under the sheer quantity of reading and the speed with which deadlines for assessed work bear down on students. Frustration can be lessened if personal reading is separated from doing assessed work, hence prolonged periods of reading for interest's sake are often best if done out of term-time. Otherwise, periods every week can be assigned, so that room is made for the work that, in many cases, caused the student to enrol on a course in the first place. Personal reading takes longer, as care tends to be taken over every word and students expect to read the whole of every text. Note-taking can be frustrating as it takes for ever, for there are no obvious guides as to what to select out. After some months of being an undergraduate people do begin to wonder if they will ever enjoy reading again.

Unfortunately deadlines come so fast, especially when students are assessed by coursework, that reading has become linked to writing assignments which will be marked. Separating reading from writing, then, in a university context is artificial as reading has become part of the means by which students are assessed, at least indirectly. While examinations still loom large, coursework assessment has become a major means of testing students and assigning final degree marks. Hence the pressure on student writing is great, and in the next chapter I look at ways of responding to students who have ceased to write or to write well enough for their own standards and their course requirements.

6

Stuck 2: Writing

People will tolerate all sorts of unhappiness at university, and a variety of problems with work. They may have lived with high levels of frustration and dissatisfaction for many months. But non-completion of written work is the trigger which makes students seek help. A phrase in common use is 'writer's block', which helps students to realize that they are not the first or only ones to meet this problem. Yet use of the phrase is unhelpful in that it gives rise to the expectation that the problem has a known antidote. Unhappily, there is no single approach, just a process of trial and error as student and study counsellor work together to find ways which ease the situation. This chapter is not philosophical about the process of writing, rather it is about these different, pragmatic, approaches which have helped to unstick the deeply stuck.

There is a daydream about writing: that it should only happen in peace, tranquillity, with country views, away from all troubles or interruptions, and with a quiet which is broken only by birds singing. It is a nice idea, but many of us have to settle for writing even though the headache is terrible, the children are screaming blue murder and the dog has thrown up on the carpet. Writing can be done in a state of tension which makes every sound a torture (especially birds singing), every ache an agonizing pain, every hunger pang experienced like the last throes of malnutrition. So tense do people become when writing that each physical sensation is experienced threefold, scalps creep with irritation, skins itch incessantly. Sometimes it is of no consequence where you write or what the distractions are, it is the state of being which needs consideration. While tranquillity is a state of mind there are many aspects of student life which make achievement of any sort of peace unlikely. Damp, crowded, unhealthy accommodation, noisy neighbours, worry about high rents all contribute to discomfort. Poor lighting, cold, sitting on the end of a bed due to lack of a table or desk, or using a torch when sharing a room is not ideal when you have to get down to some work.

A common misapprehension about academic writing, like reading, is that completion of an assignment should happen in one sitting. That is, after reading recommended material, able students write out coherent plans which, if they are sufficiently motivated, they can expand upon and write out in full. Hounsell (1984) showed that students hold different conceptions of writing, which are reflected in the strategies they develop and adopt when writing. This alternative concept, in my experience, does not stop people believing that they *ought* to write assignments 'in one go', and that their private strategies are a deviation from this ideal. Their private concepts of writing are taken by students to be signs of a deeper study problem or of a personal lack of ability. This is, of course, unhelpful nonsense.

My own hopes for student writers are:

1. that they learn to value their own approaches to writing;
2. that they learn flexibility in adopting different writing styles;
3. and that writing becomes fun.

The last hope is often the most unrealistic, as students are usually putting on an acceptable, respectable front so that they can be judged by others.

Straight lines: plans and planning

There are two reasons for writing at university: one is to use writing as a tool to aid understanding and learning; and the other is to produce a recognizably academic piece of work which is then assessed. Learning and understanding are a result of the process a student goes through, from the time a title, problem or theme is chosen to the production of a final text. This is a messy journey, starting with little understanding or apparent knowledge, exploring the sources of information, then drafting and redrafting the final version. Assessment, on the other hand, requires a polished, edited piece of writing by which students communicate to an informed reader their sense of a complex body of material and answer set questions in an acceptable form. Their work is judged, marked and criticized, all of which is experienced by students as a risky and threatening procedure.

Expecting to be able to write a complete, polished version straight off in one go stops people writing at all. Trying to write in an exploratory way while monitoring one's writing to see how it might eventually be assessed makes drafting too painful to continue. Few of us learn about writing, so we fall back on reading the end-product for inspiration about how writers write. Books are polished, edited, final versions of a project which may have taken an author years to complete. Yet students berate themselves for not being able to start at the beginning of their assignments, and write immediately in a perfectly formed, uncorrected way. The basic rule to be learnt is: you have to write badly in order to explore material, order ideas and piece together an answer. These initial experiments require polish and editing when writing a finished assignment which communicates clearly to the reader what students wish to say.

The tyranny of 'the plan' is such that all students seem to know that they are a prerequisite to producing written work. Among those who are stuck I have found that 'plans' do little except get in the way of writing. A plan can be written only when the writer knows what is going into the finished piece; it is, therefore, of no consequence to someone who is stuck, as the problem is that they manifestly do not know what to put in or how to proceed. Writing a plan can act to close down too early this essential process of exploration and clarification. Plans can act as a variation on the theme of having a perfect finished assignment formed in one's mind before starting to write, even down to individual paragraphs. Plans offer help if a student has an appointment to meet a tutor who has asked to see the student's draft or plan. Academic staff seem to be alarmed by requests for help from students who have put nothing down on paper, so it is a sign of good will on the student's part to take something to show them.

Another bad habit which the dogma of plans encourages is to be too general, talking about 'beginnings', 'middles' and 'ends', so avoiding involvement in detailed work. Like plans, this concern with the form of the final version covers up the struggle students face with: finding and reading relevant material, selecting material, organizing information, comprehending the question, understanding what is expected of them, coming up with a thesis or answer and translating into the written form the ideas visualized inside their heads. Students who own or have access to word-processors are fortunate: word-processing encourages writers to jot down ideas, move them around, insert pieces before, after and during a text. Word-processors are often recommended merely as a tool for overcoming bad handwriting or poor spelling, yet they are an excellent way of helping students to break down rigid notions of what the writing process can be like. They allow one to move sections around according to their thinking about what constitutes a 'beginning', 'middle' or 'end', which *ought* to change as they read more and write more.

What all writers need to do is engage in planning: before reading, during reading, drafting and polishing are all stages in planning routes round a question. Considering what the question means, how material relates to that question, how the writer responds to the assignment, what answers are possible, reasonable, or how they can be substantiated are all part of planning a written assignment. An important job for the tutor/counsellor, then, is to discuss writing in ways which break down this image of writing as a linear progression, and provide more constructive alternatives. Helping students to recognize that this 'mess' is, in fact, work. Learning that the activity of planning is typified by moving backwards and forwards, time and again, between the assignment title, reading, researching and one's own ideas.

Another important job for study counsellors is to find out exactly what happens to individuals whenever they sit down to write.

What worries you about writing?
What do you enjoy about writing?
How do you go about writing?

At first, responses to these questions can be quite general:

Well, I go to the library and try to do the reading.
I dunno, all of it's difficult.

Providing a detailed description requires help from the study counsellor:

Take me through this essay you're working on at the moment, the one
on toads. What's happened with that one?

Exploring the distractions which students begin to describe as obstructing progress with an assignment can be revealing. Disruptive and intrusive thoughts can be triggered by the content of the assignment. In the early 1980s I taught seminars in education studies, and the groups contained many mature students. Being intelligent, conscientious and able students, most could talk fluently on the subject of the 11+, having experienced that selection system personally. But translating their spoken words into written essays seemed impossible, and after initial enthusiasm I would have a succession of requests for deadline extensions. A colleague lent me an article by Galbraith (1980) in which he wrote of the conflict between content and form in academic writing. Using a case study of a postgraduate called 'Carolyn', Galbraith showed how one can attempt to manufacture a train of thought to satisfy readers when writing for assessment, rather than using writing as a means to pursue one's own train of thought. On this occasion the author encouraged Carolyn to focus on expressing herself rather than trying to impose an inappropriate form on her thinking, which was leaving Carolyn without any conceptual framework of her own. Applying this to my own seminars, it quickly became apparent that students were trying to squeeze a highly personal experience into what they perceived the academic form to be demanding of them. Hence their essays (when these were produced) 'hid' what they actually wished to say, were disorganized and incoherent, and they found the whole exercise dispiriting and humiliating.

In study counselling, then, a starting point with any title is to ask students for their off-the-cuff answer to a set question, which is scribbled down in six lines. This summary response may be thrown away later, if reading shows it to be inadequate. Yet time and again it metamorphoses into an acceptable academic argument. Similarly, students telling their own story of the topic to be written about is another variation of the same task. However, my education seminars taught me how deeply shamed adults feel about early school failure and problems, and care is necessary even with this seemingly innocent exercise.

A specific and individual collection of disruptive thoughts may have become linked to writing, although they are not necessarily *about* writing. They are triggered when a student sits down to write, sometimes without being aware of the repetitious nature of the thoughts, rather just conscious of the discomfort. These thoughts obliterate efforts to think deeply about an academic topic and frustrate students as they try to organize written material coherently. Instead of suppressing these thoughts, which are like half-shadows flitting across the brain, it can be helpful to draw them on a separate piece of paper, in the centre of which is the word 'essay' or 'practical' or whatever is relevant. Each thought is jotted down as it occurs, and put to one side, allowing students to draw a picture of what personal disturbances occur when writing. A series of thoughts might look like this:

> I've got to do it today.
> I didn't understand this bit yesterday.
> I'll try again.
> If I don't do it this afternoon I'll have no more time to do it.
> If I don't get it done, I'll get bad marks.
> Can I finish the course if I don't get the essays done?
> Can I do resits?
> I must get it done today.
> I don't understand this.
> If I fail, they'll be right.
> I'm stupid.
> Family – let them down.
> Family – expense of being here.
> Family – why should they care?
> Family – I wish they'd get off my back.
> Family – what right do they have to complain?
> I must get it done today.

The tutor/counsellor's role is to help students to move away from negative descriptions, such as 'I can't concentrate' or 'I can't organize material', and to work out instead what is actually *happening*. Establishing positive definitions of what occurs helps students take the initiative in bringing about change and makes it clearer to students and counsellor the exact nature of their writing problems. Students frequently stop writing at a difficult point, and return to it at the same point of tension, which stirs up a sense of defeat similar to the one felt when last leaving a piece of work. Eventually, just thinking of writing can be a sufficient trigger to invite all these depressing feelings. Resolutely sitting on such thoughts and trying to drive oneself forward is wearing, as students clench their teeth and grip pens, and sit for hours in an uncomfortable state of tension. This makes the whole process far more difficult to sustain for long periods and is physically unpleasant for one's back. It can be interesting to see which thoughts cause most disruption, and to realize how integrated into the whole of life the process of writing is.

Talking it out

People who mark students' writing are often disappointed that writers have not critically assessed and analysed material, and they look for clarity of intent, purpose or cohesion in the critical argument put forward. Writers should have an argument, a solution to offer or an answer to give, for no academic essay question in any discipline will say: 'Tell me all you know about . . .'. A hallmark of an educated person may, in Western society, be an ability to opine fluently on a range of topics, but most of us have to scrabble between the jigsaw pieces of new information to make sense of it first. Faced with a new writing assignment, most do not experience a rush of fully formed opinion, more a wave of terror. When reading, any embryonic views get buried under an avalanche of expert opinion. It takes a lot of work and practice to hear your own voice and to piece together an argument which you, the writer, can respect.

Writers are usually told to start with the title and examine what it is asking, but most of us do not really know how to go about this sort of analysis. If already stuck or confused, then analysing an assignment title may add to difficulties, as students tie their brains in knots trying to semantically separate 'contrast' from 'compare', 'assess' from 'evaluate'. Like Carolyn, in Galbraith's example, students can find that they have nothing to say at all on occasion and experience a terrible blankness of mind. A more holistic approach to the title, starting with one's broad responses to it, is more productive, with fine-tuning and detailed analysis coming later. A holistic response does not mean attempting to come up with an immediate answer, rather it means allowing your mind to take a walk around the topic, translating one question into a series of questions, which will provide a basis for active reading. Imagine an essay title went something like:

> Assess the view that the values associated with fundamentalist religious convictions are the same as those which ensured the success of right-wing politics in the United States in the 1980s.

A list of questions would look like this:

> What are values?
> What are fundamentalist religious convictions?
> What are fundamentalist values?
> What are right-wing values supposed to be?
> What's the story of US politics in the 1980s?
> Who holds that view, and what do they argue?
> What is their evidence?
> What do they miss out?
> What does not ring true in their argument?
> Who argues the opposite – what do they say and what is their evidence?
> Does it ring true?
> If not, why not?

Students think they know nothing about a subject until they have read up on it, yet they have attended lectures, seminars or done previous courses which touch on the topic. Dragging up anything from the back of the brain which seems relevant helps clear one's mind before reading complex material. A mind-game has to be played which is a close relative of 'brain-storming' anything that comes to mind, to squeeze this information out from the back of people's brains. The difference is that ideas may not flow, they might trickle, and one must learn the technique of taking perhaps only one word and teasing out where it has come from. While some people enjoy writing this down in any order, others prefer a 'shopping-list' style: the counsellor's role is to gently draw out a list of this kind, joining in by racking their own brain (without shame at displaying their own ignorance). The intention is to start work by breaking down the title conceptually rather than beginning with the semantics of question construction.

This list can be written in felt-tip pens, on large paper attached to the wall, and stay there while students get on with some reading. The list can become a series of headings: even if the final text does not require head-ings, there is no reason why a writer cannot use them when drafting (espe-cially if organization of material presents the writer with special problems). Headings can be removed when proof-reading as one checks how well or badly one section flows into the next. Items on the list can act as a focus for 'free' writing: allowing ten minutes to scribble down anything that seems relevant under that heading. Using a pencil is a comfortable way of releas-ing the tension attached to 'neat' writing, and short-circuits the desire to produce the 'best' copy first. Word-processors serve a similar function in allowing one to separate the technical aspects of manuscript production from the exploration of ideas and material. For those who work with pens and paper, early drafts can be cut up with scissors and moved around while considering why one section should follow another, what argument links them together and what more needs to be inserted to provide coherence.

These varied means of translating the spoken word into early written drafts do not occur chronologically, rather students move backwards and forwards between writing and reading, or between writing and research, building up a picture, changing the picture, adding to their original under-standing. As ideas begin to flow more easily, it becomes less daunting for students to attend more closely to the exact detail of what an assignment title is asking of them. A study counsellor's role is to support students while they experiment with different ways of writing academically, to foster per-sonal styles and habits, and to help track down what styles of working suit a student best. A popular device used is the 'spider diagram' which encour-ages people to 'brainstorm', then to link the ideas with coloured pens. There are those for whom it adds to the confusion. They may find it useful to use coloured pens and flip-chart paper to 'play' with ideas, but find linking them in the spider diagram manner too confusing. One-to-one work may include spending time building up people's confidence sufficiently to allow them to dump plans and diagrams if they prove unhelpful, and replace them with ways of planning which suit them better.

What is expected of student writers?

Polishing and shaping one's writing to fit the particular medium has to be worked at after writing has started again. However, Hounsell (1984: 30) has argued that talking about the *means* of writing is 'of limited usefulness if it fails to confront an inappropriate grasp of what is meant by an essay'. Understanding what the constraints of the medium are makes it easier for some students to restart writing as the mystique is removed, leaving, one hopes, a human-sized exercise; and it helps to make it clearer why editing and exploration are different stages of drafting.

A part of the terror of being assessed lies in not knowing what finished academic work should look like. Students may have only a vague notion of what is expected of them as writers, and have no sense of purpose when writing other than meeting a general requirement that they should present themselves for judgement. Writing is seen only as a means by which 'they' check up that students are working, and it can feel as if it is the writer not the work which is being assessed. The rules by which they are judged are not clear to all students, whatever cues are given out by tutors or fellow students, and tutor/counsellors need to help students build up a personal sense of what is formally expected of them as academic writers.

Academic writing is, like any other medium, a highly contrived activity. It has its own rules and etiquette about what is acceptable writing behaviour and what is not. I would like people to graduate with sufficient writing skills to be able to adjust according to what they wish to achieve: able to write technical reports but with awareness of how that differs from writing plays. Approaching academic writing as just one form of communication among many is a means of encouraging flexibility in writing styles. Some have not had to write academically at all since they were in their early teens. It is possible for students to take a science route at this point and arrive at university via BTEC courses or HNDs, and so have no concept of what a university essay looks like. It can take some time and work to help such people develop a rudimentary concept of what they are working towards. In addition to talking about styles of academic writing, effort needs to go into finding sources which give clues about academic writing. Some sources to use for rudimentary analysis are:

- Books: five minutes before reading items from the reading list to think about how the introduction (to chapters as well as to the book) is dealt with and to examine the author's style.
- Lecturers' styles in putting lectures together vary considerably: some will break all data down under headings, and some will approach material in a more discursive style.
- Friends' successful essays: for structure not content.
- Students' own essays: analysing essays which have received different marks and looking, in detail, at why essays got the marks they did, and using lecturers' comments (when they exist) to help pick out the mark-earning habits from the mark-losing ones.

Analysing other sources for clues sounds good, but it is not always obvious what this might mean in practice. In individual sessions I find it helpful to compose a list of questions students see as most useful. A list of questions could include:

1. What's the overall shape – how does the writer deal with the beginning, middle and end?
2. What does the introduction do? Does it lay out what's coming, does it summarize, offer background/context, or what?
3. How is data dealt with and presented, and what constitutes data?
4. What do the conclusions add to the piece?
5. What sort of language is used? Is anything striking about it?
6. What is the central theme – could you summarize it?
7. Trace the central theme through. How is it explored?

Students assume that they write 'wrongly' and know little of value about academic writing. Exercise 6.1 can be used with individual students or in groups, and avoids putting adults 'on the spot' by making them confess that they do not know what is expected of them.

Exercise 6.1: The worst way of writing

In groups, compose a list of instructions which describe the *worst* possible way of producing an essay/laboratory report/literary review.

The commonest form of academic writing, and the most energy-consuming, is the traditional essay, and students need to be clear about the length of essay expected, the deadline, referencing, and what the title means. An essay asks writers: to research complex material; to make sense of that material; and then communicate that understanding of complex data to an informed reader. A writer communicates understanding via a thesis or argument, in answer to a set question. Anything that hinders communication – poor handwriting, illogical or confused ordering of evidence, bad spelling – is likely to be penalized. It is not, however, the only form of writing by which students are assessed, and tutor/counsellors need to be sure that their own assumptions about what is being asked of student writers are accurate. Most of all, study counsellors should not take their original courses of study as undergraduates as blueprints for what is expected.

Exercise 6.2 can be used with either staff or students in workshops. It is deliberately simple, and is intended to produce answers that are not hidden in codes or assumptions. For those who are successful academically, it is not enough to have a 'feel' for their form of writing, as if this somehow comes naturally. Successful academics as well as students need to be able to make explicit what constitutes 'success' by being able to clarify the purposes and nature of writing tasks. Exercise 6.3, in the next section, asks staff and students to define writing styles either in groups from their 'home' department or to make comparisons within mixed groups.

Exercise 6.2: What is involved in writing at university?

For staff and students: take three of the many writing tasks set at university and discuss them in relation to the following questions:

- What are the purposes in writing?
- What is the length and structure expected in an assessable text?
- What is distinctive about an essay, say, compared with another academic writing task?
- What will earn good marks?
- What will earn bad marks?

Disciplines and variety

Students who take subjects from different disciplines can be confused by variations in style between apparently related subjects. As we have already seen in Chapter 5, Becher's work presents disciplines and their practitioners as quite different in their styles of work, and lecturers on interdisciplinary courses can have fixed ideas of academic excellence which spring from their 'home' discipline. Students feel as if they are being messed about just for the fun of it, and become more and more dependent on the good opinion of markers for any sense of achievement. This means looking out for cues in a highly instrumental way. While many students take this for granted as a fact of academic life, others find this approach sufficiently distressing to stop them working. 'How to do a degree' books can provoke similar distress in people who wanted more depth of learning from a degree than cynically manipulating a system of marking. Students who are looking for some personal satisfaction from study feel so frustrated by the 'game' element that their capacity to continue working breaks down completely. Using reading as a means of gaining insight into these variations between subjects and between disciplines can lessen the sense of being bounced off the walls by what appear, at first sight, to be mindless variations. This has obvious benefits when it comes to students learning to write flexibly and appropriately.

Variations of expression between disciplines (and between subjects within disciplines) are rarely accidental, rather they reflect differences of approach to scholarship. To people who have been professional sociologists for half a lifetime, their brand of writing may have become second nature, and it is this writing code which students have to crack. Students are faced with the job of producing a piece of writing that the marker recognizes as sociology, history, biology or whatever. One approach is to encourage people to 'describe what a psychology essay is' (or whatever subject they are studying). The kinds of description they come up with might be like this:

S: Well, they want you to put loads of experiments in.

M: What do you have to do with the experiments?

S: I dunno, show that you know them.

M: How long is the essay, what does it look like?

S: It's short, only about 1500 words. The tutor said he wants head-ings, he doesn't want it just rambling on.

M: So what's 'rambling' in these essays?

S: Oh, you know, your own opinion, analysis, that kind of stuff.

M: So it's fairly descriptive?

S: Yeah, that's right, they just want the facts down under headings, with your conclusions at the end, no padding.

M: Right, so it's short, pithy, descriptive, based on other people's experiments?

S: Yeah.

M: So what are these headings?

S: Well, it's like a lab report, they want hypothesis, experiments and conclusions, but in this case you use the books to find out about the experiments instead of doing it yourself.

Exercise 6.3 was originally designed for staff to use, but can also be done with small groups of experienced students. For any team of staff setting up an interdisciplinary course, this exercise is an interesting focus for discus-sion about official expectations of student performance. If used within one department this can, of course, be a precursor to agreeing what can reason-ably be expected of first-year students, especially if there is a range of tutors and markers working together for the first time. The intention is not to produce model answers, but to assess general expectations about style, use of data, arguments, and so on.

Exercise 6.3: Getting rid of the mystique

Write a number of introductory paragraphs in answer to some first-year essay ques-tions (taken from last year). Write one excellent one, one reasonable one, one averagely acceptable one and one bad one. Do not go overboard or produce something which is intentionally funny: assume that the student is writing seriously, and trying to write a reasonable essay.

If this is in a mixed workshop, staff from different departments can opt to take different levels of writing (for example, geography – excellent, politics – bad, accountancy – acceptable, and biology – reasonable). At the end, they must explain and record what elements in a paragraph make it achieve that standard, and what this says about their subject/discipline. If an inter-disciplinary course is under discussion then participants must try to produce *one* agreed list covering these points.

If the workshop participants come from the same department then different groups can opt to take different levels (group 1 – excellent, and so on), but they must then go through the same process of explaining to other groups what elements of the paragraph earned or lost marks and what this says about the discipline.

I keep a selection of 'introductory paragraphs' for use in individual sessions to raise awareness of these issues, and naturally none are precisely right for any discipline. But they serve to act as a focus for discussion and 'awareness-raising':

(a) The cats rushed towards me through a hole in the wall of the abandoned building. They came at such speed that I could only distinguish the colour of the large ginger tom who came first. After that a blur of tabby fur, yellow, black and white and dirty moggies yowled and fought their way through, pausing not at all and hissing with rage as they made good their escape.

(b) We established our observation point in front of the site which we had already established was home to a colony of cats (Fang 1966). Our intention was to count the number of cats in the colony and to record the number of colour types. One enumerator waited in front of the cats' main means of egress (see Aniel 1967), while a second caused an alarm sufficient to oblige the cats to evacuate their home. We discovered three difficulties with this method of research, as yet unrecorded in the literature (see, for example, Dogg *et al.* 1960): first, the rate of the subjects' egress was such that counting could not be accurate; second, their speed made colour-distinction an impossible task; and third, even had they moved more slowly, it would not have been possible to both count and distinguish colour variations in a systematic way.

References

Aniel, S.P. (1967) 'Cat colonies: safety in mono-egress environments' in *Behavioural Psychoterminology and the Modern Mog*, 50 (4) pp. 670–902.

Dogg, A., Mutt, K. and Hound, D. (1960) 'Hand grenades and action research', *Canine Defence and Research Quarterly*, 15 (9) pp. 234–543.

Fang, S. (1966) *Feline Aspirations: Hypothesis Building from Observation* (1st Interim Report), Centre for Research into Canine Defence, N.Y.

Clarifying understanding of the medium through which academic thoughts are expressed helps students to build bridges between a highly personal understanding of a topic and communicating that understanding publicly. Increased awareness of language use in one's chosen discipline takes people away from a sense of being at the mercy of arbitrary forces, and closer to taking control of the terms on which they engage in assessment procedures.

Finishing off

The final written text is a means of communication between a student and a representative of an academic readership, the tutor who marks the essay. The finished product must look like what passes for communication within that discipline, and it must also communicate, which requires clarity. There are two sorts of clarity students need to consider when 'proof-reading': one is clarity of communication, which refers to intelligibility, legibility, spelling, coherence and consistency in language use; and the other is clarity of meaning, which is being clear about the thesis or answer offered, why the substantiating data is laid out in the way chosen, and whether the finished text is organized in a way which makes convincing sense to the reader.

There are no short-cuts to improvement for native English speakers who have profound problems with language use and construction. My approach to helping someone to write *at all* if faced with severe language problems is: to concentrate first on clear understanding of the topic, an unstructured approach to writing a draft answer, followed by translation into a simple structure using simple language. By separating out the stages in writing even more deliberately than usual, students can experiment with their approaches to writing while 'buying time' in which to improve language use.

I have never found it helpful to start work on the construction and use of language with students whose capacity to work has crumbled. But where there are basic language problems, then they will need to be addressed, and whatever the student's understanding it will take time and practice before signs of improvement show. Sadly, those students will become greatly confused as different members of staff lay down with equal force quite conflicting rules of grammar and punctuation. Those of us who had 'grammar' battered into our heads seem to have an emotional commitment to believing that what we were taught is the only correct use of English and allow little leeway for argument. Carey wrote of punctuation with humour and incisiveness in 1939, and updated his pithy book in 1958, in which he commented that punctuation is a mixture of taste and rules:

> I should define punctuation as being governed two-thirds by rule and one-third by personal taste. I shall endeavour not to stress the former to the exclusion of the latter, but I will not knuckle under to those who apparently claim for themselves complete freedom to do what they please in the matter. (Carey 1971: 13)

Every generation appears to feel that they were the last to be taught 'proper' English and see punctuation as a sign of all the evils which bedevil their world. One wishes to progress, but without spelling, language structure and use to be attached to all these emotive matters. But the academic medium is a means of communication and academic writers, however new, need to keep to some of the rules of its ilk.

People need to start by learning the rudiments of proof-reading, to apply to the work they are producing. I do not find it helpful to give students proof-reading exercises to do on their own until it is obvious they are comfortable with them and do not take them too seriously. Instead, I prefer to do one occasionally with them. Working together in a light-hearted way gives the opportunity to draw out and reinforce underlying rules where these exist. Word-processors make it easy to generate your own pieces of proof-reading text from your own writing, rather than mutilating other people's work. The principles are: the text should be clear and easy to read, with extra gaps if necessary to encourage ease of reading. The object is not to catch students out with unusual or difficult language, but to encourage the habit of assessing a text rapidly for obvious errors.

Recommending books to help students with these aspects of writing is not always successful: instead, browsing through bookshops and libraries with the intention of finding ones that feel attractive is a better starting point for people. Books on English as a foreign language are more likely to present basic matters to adults in a clear and unpatronizing way. My own favourite for adults who wish to improve their style is Sir Ernest Gowers's *The Complete Plain Words* (1979), mainly for its humility and emphasis on using simple, direct language with the intention of communicating to the reader. Originally published in two parts (*Plain Words* in 1948, and *The ABC of Plain Words* in 1951) which were brought together in one volume in 1954, it has gone through numerous reprints and two revisions. Gowers's work is clear yet allows for the complexities of language use and developments over time. Reading is one of the most effective means of improving fluency with English, whether it be reading from magazines or from classic novels.

Encouraging students to hand in written work for assessment when they have only just started to write again is difficult. On rare occasions I have acted as a 'bank' for completed work, so that the terror of giving work to a department can be separated from the process of writing. This emergency measure delays the inevitable, which is excruciating torture for some students. Sadly, the joy of producing written work which is awarded a pass mark can be wiped out by careless comments from tutors who incautiously rail against simple structures and styles. Fortunately, not all lecturers respond this way, and many understand the need to explain what students have done well alongside suggesting ways for future improvement. But students do perceive constructive criticism as devastating and they ignore positive comments while taking in only critical statements. It is a tutor's job to offer constructive criticism, and one part of my role is to help students learn to make use of good criticism while discounting the careless. One approach is to concentrate on recording what an individual student has got out of a writing task, regardless of institutional assessments. I find it helpful to have a handout prepared which allows students to think quietly about their own assessments, without my voice in their ears. These same questions can be explored in individual meetings, particularly if students are shocked by marks vastly different (better or worse) than they were expecting.

What mark would I give this work?
What are the best aspects of this work?
What are the weaker parts?
What has satisfied me most in preparing this work?
What would I do differently next time?

Self-assessment is not helpful for every student. While we all experience discomfort when being assessed, the degrees to which different people feel upset by the process varies. Some feel distressed, others feel devastated, and it is not enough to respond by saying 'we all feel like that', for it may not be true. Time and space are needed to explore exactly what it does feel like for *this* person when assessed writing is returned, for what is a good mark for one is the onset of terror for another. Any form of communication is an act of offering yourself, your experience and your world-view for the judgement of others. In the next chapter I look more closely at the myriad ways in which the adult 'self' and academic work interact.

7

Talking 2: Self and Communication

A study counsellor works alongside students as they ask a variety of spoken and unspoken questions. In the first stages of 'stuckness' people want to know how to get out of a crisis, how to stop feeling so bad. But as bad feelings lessen, so the questions change.

How do I understand better how I got into this, what do I want my academic life to be like?
How do I get from where I am now to where I'd like to be?

For students of counselling the notion of 'stuckness' has many resonances, and while crisis management and improvement may be experienced as different stages of questioning, exploring answers to both sets of questions is part of the same journey. Academic work means different things to different people. Its role in life varies from student to student. What meaning it holds for an individual's life cannot be guessed at, but has to be worked out carefully, in a joint enterprise taking some time and patience, where progress may be slow. While there are many study techniques which can be taught and used effectively, the answers to these questions always remain highly personal and individualized.

So, for example, it does not matter how successful everyone else judges students to be as long as their own self-esteem remains low. The world appears to see academic success as worthwhile and desirable (up to a point), so it can be hard to understand the owners of A and B grades at A level or other highly prized qualifications when they are trying to say that they are not truly lovable, and certainly not clever, and that they really do feel distressed by academic work. 'Feeling bad' is experienced as shameful and hard to confess to, and also, paradoxically, as so self-evident that it needs no explanation. But it does require discussion, because bad to one is not the same as bad to another, and 'not being able to do essays' or 'not being able to deal with reading' are not statements which, without elaboration, tell one much about what is actually going on.

M: Talk me through how you go about writing an essay.

S: I just get the title, go to the library and then I take too long, it takes me for ever.

M: How do you choose a title?

S: I don't know. I just choose whatever looks easiest. If we've already had a lecture or a seminar, or I've done something similar before.

M: (mental note – no breaking new ground, is 'difficult' seen as 'impossible'?) What's 'easiest' for you?

S: If I've already heard the lecturer say something, what it's about, so I've got an idea what the right track is. You can write for ever and be doing the wrong stuff.

M: (taking risks is not an option) What do you do if you don't know what the right track is?

S: Well, it's impossible, it takes for ever, you don't know what to select out of the reading, what to include. It's not fair really, I think they should give you some idea, a handout or something. How are you supposed to know otherwise?

M: So, tell me how you go about doing essays.

S: I don't have a system. I just get the essay title and go to the library, then I get stuck.

M: Which bit do you get stuck with?

S: Well, the reading, of course. I never know what to take notes on. I end up photocopying it all. I just feel so bad when I sit there with the book in front of me.

M: What does bad feel like?

S: I dunno. Just like the inside of my head's disappearing down a plughole.

M: So, tell me how you go about doing essays.

S: I don't have a system. I just get the essay title and go to the library, then I get stuck.

M: Which bit do you get stuck with?

S: Well, it's before I get there really. You can't get any books from the library. I wake up in a cold sweat early in the morning, I'm really scared there'll be no books left. I just have to look at the library doors these days to start feeling sick.

M: So, tell me how you go about doing essays.

S: I just get the essay title and go to the library, then I get stuck.

M: Which bit do you get stuck with?

S: It's with the essay title. I think I've chosen one, but really I haven't. I start work on one, then I think a different one might be easier, so I start getting the books for that. Then I think I should stick with the first one, then I just panic.

M: What does panic mean for you?

S: It's like, I want to cry, but you can't cry in the library, then I get shaky, then all hell breaks lose.

M: What's 'all hell'?

S: It's, like, I panic that I'm going to do something stupid, lose control. This wave of terror just wells up and hits me, like I'm disintegrating. It's like having a temperature, I get all hot and clammy, but I think something dreadful's going to happen to me there and then. I haven't been back to the library since last time.

Whatever happens with study, the underlying desire may be to stop feeling this bad so often. Developing academically may be one set of issues, but another might be: 'How do I live with these reactions to study and do those things which I want to do?'

How people feel about themselves and life can be enmeshed with study; writing, in particular, is an activity which can reach down inside and find the sensitive parts. As well as communicating academic aspects of ourselves, the process of learning communicates about other, sometimes less constructive, elements of our lives. This can be so whatever the medium, whether painting, music, laboratory reports, mathematical theorems, fiction, computer programs or essay writing. Where communication with others, particularly, has been inhibited, shaped or influenced by life in unconstructive ways, then this may well express itself through academic work. So, for example, an essential ingredient in depression is low self-esteem and a history of having been told what a bad person you are. Taking part in the stressful exercise of complex academic work coupled with impersonal assessment procedures can trigger off unhappy resonances which a study counsellor has to work alongside. Pressures bring sadnesses, angers and griefs bubbling to the surface, making difficult academic tasks even harder. Other forms of communication are exposed, other relationships are put on the line. McLoughlin (1990: 63) summarizes the phenomena of transference and countertransference as terms which describe how both parties in a counselling relationship can transfer 'feelings and conflicts which belong somewhere else' on to their meetings. A study counsellor needs to work with students sufficiently to enable them to achieve their academic goals, before they have necessarily unravelled the hurt and depression they experience. These feelings are all the more frightening when they have become coupled with academic work, because students have no idea of where the feelings are coming from, what they are about, or where these feelings really belong. Only rarely have they heard of others undergoing this amount of distress while undergraduates.

Family relationships

Our relationship with learning reflects prior relationships with authoritative and powerful figures. Responses to matters of attainment and achievement carry echoes of family relationships, parental hopes and partners' lives, and what achievement has meant in our relationships with all of them. Sartre (1964: 97) describes a childhood enmeshed in the printed and written word, powerfully shadowed by his grandfather. It was a childhood he loathed, and he wrote to escape the shoddy and empty liar he knew himself to be, elaborating the lies. 'By writing, I existed, I escaped from the grown-ups; but I existed only to write and if I said: me – that meant the me who wrote.' The child Sartre used writing as part of his double life, protecting the private. Where the resonances and meanings of writing in a life are so profound, then the act of stopping writing also implies profundity. Similarly, the role which 'being academic' has taken in students' lives can be complex and have meanings for their sense of self well beyond getting a job or pleasing parents, though both of these may also be true. The distress of not producing written assignments, for example, is so much greater if it represents the end of a belief in one's own existence, as academic expression can symbolize.

'Being clever' is a useful retreat for children, a means of backing away from family relationships with which they cannot cope. This is clearer with activities such as playing computer games, and not so obvious when it involves success at schoolwork and those means by which we define 'good' children. When cleverness becomes the only means of expressing oneself, the only recognizable passage to the future, then one is always facing potential danger. For ideas, writing and the capacity to solve mathematical equations can be transient or temporary ephemera, sometimes they happen and sometimes they do not, and they cannot fill every minute of the day and night. One cannot understand everything, nor can one always produce new, original thoughts. The pressure which comes from establishing a sense of self by these routes *alone* is terrible. Assessment at university is difficult for most people to cope with, and there is pain in being marked in a seemingly uncaring system. But if one's whole sense of being and source of worth is attached to the marks received then the process of being a student is potentially overwhelming.

A study counsellor listening to concerns apparently about tutors and assessment should sense these echoes, and may well find they are hearing about parents, powerful teachers and the re-enactment of old hurts. Some histories are painful, and are the age-old stories of adults' brutality to children. For many mature students, educated in the 1940s and 1950s, one consequence of failure at school was high levels of violence from teachers within schools. This was so much the wallpaper of school life that it is barely remembered, yet the anxiety about the consequences of being seen to be less than perfect lives on. Our belief that the intellect is separate from the emotional self makes it harder to remember and accurately 'place' the feelings where they belong, hence easy to retain belief in one's irrationality and incapability.

It is usually assumed that successfully completed work is a desirable goal, yet there are ways in which academic success triggers internal punishments. So, for example, writing essays requires students to state their thesis or argument. While everyone insists that 'young people today' are encouraged to state their opinions on everything, in fact many have experienced punishment for expressing their view. This is easier to recognize in the past, where physical punishment might have occurred for children with opinions; however, withdrawal of love for thinking children takes many forms. Families wish their children to do well at school and in life, but may actually disapprove of their children spending too much time in books and subtly communicate this, resulting in guilty feelings at time spent this way rather than on activities which are more easily accepted as appropriate in the family.

The course content itself can be threatening, particularly religious or political views which stand in opposition to the beliefs held in the family home, and even discussion of 'deviant' ideas can be experienced by a student as disloyalty. Study counsellors are likely to meet individuals who have been subject to physical violence or sexual abuse while growing up, or violence from current partners. Academic work can provide a mental escape route from abuse and the intellect may have become a tool to assist in distancing oneself mentally from pain. This is a powerful process of dissociation, and Renvoize (1993: 145) has described how some victims imagine themselves at a distance from the body undergoing abuse or use their mind to pretend that the part of themselves being violated does not, in fact, exist. This form of blockage is highly effective, and the habit of using the brain to numb sensation and emotion becomes a problem if emotions and sensations later begin to seep out through academic activity. In some households, doing one's homework can represent a precious occasion on which boundaries between adults and children are clear, and they have a sense of their own being, uninvaded. This level of escapism requires academic work to be safe and predictable, and is resistant to playing with new approaches to study. If childhood abuse or domestic violence are also topics to be studied, then work becomes a lightning conductor for deeply felt emotions (albeit not always acknowledged feelings). On occasion, then, study counsellors will be aware that reflecting on the process of learning may, for an individual student, remove a screen hiding greater horrors.

Describing students' experiences as 'doing what parents expect' gags clients and stops them experiencing the real impact of their independent, intellectual selves. Most people will share values with their families and wish to please them, and attending university can be a matter of pride for families (not, however, all families). But university is the way of leaving home, and this brings about changes in families – albeit via a route encouraged by families. Hence students move on to 'own' the independent self and combine family values with new thoughts, ideas and behaviour peculiarly their own. And so academic work can, unawares, become a flashpoint for family conflict. There are students whose work deteriorates regularly rather than just in a specific crisis, during vacations spent at home with their families, and with whom a full term can go by working to recover the academic ground thereby lost. They lose the capacity to think straight or hear their own inner voices, and such students suffer from what I call 'invasive' families.

The intellectual self may, by the student's full ownership of it, be a cause of tension in the family. Exactly what role did getting to university play in the family: a sign of childly obedience by completing homework quietly night after night? A sign of 'success' in parenthood, by not spending time on drugs, drink or car theft? Does it mean, we wanted our daughter to be a credit to us, but not too much so? Does it mean, I am afraid my wife is growing away from me? Does it mean there is no real room in your household for an adult with independent thoughts, whose intellectual life is acceptable to the rest of the family?

Cultural and social values

Undergraduates absorb social values like anyone else growing up in the world. These values have an impact on the role of academic endeavour in any individual's life. On the surface the belief that it is good to be academically successful seems uncomplicated. But the social and class pressures on any one individual, often mediated through the family, to conform to roles which do not include academic success are great. All who undergo university study – whether aged 18 or 80 – are likely to develop and change in ideas, outlook, confidence and expectations of life. However, this process of change is experienced as more destructive and painful by some than by others, and 'not knowing your place' can become intimately intertwined with academic work. Confusion arises as mixed messages are transmitted and received, and people experience social sanctions for academic success as well as rewards, for they are transgressing social and familial codes. For example, a person may be sincerely aggrieved when accused of not wanting their student partner to do a degree. While genuinely not objecting to this aim, a spouse will have expected degree work to fit in rather like a hobby, which can be dropped easily for more pressing matters, like visiting family or friends. If the huge changes study brings about in individuals are not acknowledged by their families and partners then undergraduate study does, indeed, threaten that family structure. An extreme example of mixed messages is the couple in which one partner is reportedly highly supportive of their student partner, up until the time when divorce becomes the only means of resolving the tensions brought about by change.

   Academic endeavour is not culturally neutral: even in 1968, apparently the height of liberal tolerance among intellectuals, Leach (1968: 15) acknowledged that British universities are designed to inculcate individuals in 'the manners and accomplishments of an elderly Cambridge don of the male sex'. The aims and purposes of universities always come under discussion at times of change and such debate reflects the social values which underpin both the system and subject content of higher education. This was no less so in the nineteenth century than it is now, when the ancient English universities had traditionally acted as the training grounds for professions of the Church and the Civil Service. Sanderson (1975: 207–8) explains how Joseph Chamberlain intended Birmingham 'to do for industrial training what the older universities already did for the professions', and hence established departments of brewing, metallurgy and the like. But, as the Scottish universities had found with the reformed Civil Service examinations, Oxford and Cambridge remained supreme and their syllabuses formed the basis of these new examinations. The Oxford and Cambridge model did not, according to Sanderson (1975: 4), transfer easily to newer universities, linked, as it was, with a class structure, and in the newer institutions, where students were drawn from other social classes, they 'found such curricula totally unsuitable for their needs'. The traditionally close links between civic universities and their communities do not always continue to be valued in their modern forms. The Nobel Prize-winning scientist, Sir Peter Medawar, has written of how he objected to the open day held at the University of Birmingham, where he moved from Oxford to become professor of zoology in 1947. Medawar (1988: 104) felt the public took little in as they viewed exhibits 'perhaps because they were haunted by the fear that they might miss the free tea which had been billed as part of the proceedings'.

The links between social class and the study of applied subjects implied in Sanderson's account adds another dimension to the belief that universities should only concern themselves with learning for its own sake. Doubts surrounding the 'impurity' of applied research were voiced by Bertrand Russell, who otherwise happily accepted the universities' role in training professionals. A believer in the possibility of an 'educated democracy', Russell (1976: 197–8) wanted public rather than private funds to enable pure research to continue unimpeded by concerns of money, and saw learning as suffering when learned men earned money by applying themselves to 'teaching brewing instead of organic chemistry'.

It is unlikely that Russell envisaged the expansion of universities on quite the scale which was to follow, but greater provision of university places has led to calls for improved applicability of graduates' skills in the world of work, rather than a wider acceptance of the value of pure research. But negative judgements about the value of different university courses continue to be made. What, at one level, is a debate about the purposes of university education is, at another, a part of the social values which allow students to see themselves as not really academic at all, in spite of their qualifications. Doing apparently 'unfashionable' subjects in 'unfashionable' places allows one to become depressed in the face of study problems – I always knew I was stupid and this just goes to prove it.

Wider access to university education has seen the development of a hierarchy of subjects, a pecking order which includes concepts of 'hard' and 'soft' subjects. The entry of women into universities in substantial numbers in the latter half of the twentieth century has shown that subject choice reflects wider gender divisions within society, and women students are concentrated in those subjects perceived as 'soft'. Thomas (1990: 179) argues that higher education 'does not actively discriminate against women; rather, through an acceptance of particular values and beliefs, it makes it difficult for women to succeed'; for social values prevalent in the rest of the world impact upon university communities, too. Up to university many girls have been 'good' by achieving at school, now they are moving into those grey areas where being academically good may be seen as sex-inappropriate and an underlying lack of confidence becomes more pronounced (Peelo 1988). Mature students, in particular, know the undermining sense of believing themselves to be frauds, and students can carry a secret explanation as to how they were mistakenly allowed into university:

> I was lucky with the interviewer.
> They let anyone into these new universities.
> The department was being experimental that year.
> I'm a good talker.
> The standards aren't so high these days.
> They're desperate to get students to come here.
> I had good teaching on my access course.
> I've been lucky up to now with the questions/markers.
> I think they had a place left over.

Students live with the permanent expectation of being 'rumbled' as stupid, incapable of doing degree work, so any lapse from a first-class standard is experienced as proof of deeper deficiencies rather than as an occasional hiccup. Even though mature students hear each other describe anxious feelings, they can still feel isolated as the only undergraduate who is, secretly, quite so inappropriate for a university place.

Anxiety about work can result from being pulled in two equally strong directions at one and the same time, wanting to succeed in work while suffering punishment through loss of cultural security. While good children succeed academically, this success can set them on a social path which produces tension with family and friends. Sivanandan's (1974: 104) haunting description of the 'coloured' intellectual is of one adrift in 'a world of false shadows and false light', forever caught between two worlds. Becoming a successful student is experienced painfully by some students as the process of becoming white, and being tied in a strait-jacket of other people's vocabulary, their meanings and their culture. It is commonplace now to talk of the successes of the old grammar school system, but Jackson and Marsden (1968: 177) found some working-class children for whom academic success led to a lack of familial closeness, and describe the subsequent, real, pain of a 'drifting, rudderless existence'.

The power of 'educated' language to separate one out within one's known world is described by the playwright, Hugh Leonard, in one volume of his autobiography. Aware, in his teens, of some need to show that his scholarship and books had not made him 'too big for his boots', he went along to play 'housey-housey' with his adoptive father. Leonard made a fool of himself by asking for a 'board' instead of a 'card'. His father, unaware of the cause

of the laughter, joined in the mirth. In his play, *A Life*, he gave these words
to Desmond Drumm to describe his humiliation:

> I understood. It was a punishment. I had broken the eleventh com-
> mandment. I had tried to be different, to be a clever boy, the born
> genius. Well, they were not impressed. I had discovered that clever-
> ness was like having a deformed hand. It was tolerated as long as you
> kept a glove on it. (Leonard 1989: 125)

As Leonard indicates, doing well academically can be about 'getting above
yourself' socially. Students receive mixed messages as families impose sanctions for 'being too clever by half' and make them the butt of family jokes,
which border on humiliation. Rowe (1991: 228) writes that the Australian
equivalent of 'too clever by half' is 'tall poppies', which have to be cut down
as they stand above other plants in the field. Keeping one member in his
or her 'proper' place maintains the shaky esteem of powerful figures unable
to cope with close relatives' abilities and cements a family in pre-university
relationships. Whatever it achieves, this cutting down will be presented as
affectionate teasing, and students, naturally, find it hard to recognize when
there is destructive envy within the circle of those who apparently love
them.

Social class has not only underpinned who goes to university and who
does not, it has shaped individuals' assessments of their own abilities. White
(1986: 109) describes how, even though he understood the impact of social
class on his life, when a tutor suggested he apply to university, his reaction
was to say 'degrees are for clever people and not for the likes of me'.
Letting go of poor childhood performance is not easy if one has also been
brought up to believe that lack of ability is an integral part of you, like
personality or eye colour. Being judged to have written an assignment worth
40 per cent, therefore, means being a 40 per cent person. Teachers correct
social aspects of classroom behaviour as well as academic work, and many
grew up knowing that their poverty and dirtiness came from the same
source as their innate stupidity as exposed by the 11+ examination. A low
mark at university brings the same sense of shame as being discovered as
'dirty' when a primary school child.

Internal standards

I offer solace and comfort as these matters bubble and surface, but it is not
my role to challenge troubled students with social and family issues. Rather,
awareness of their importance allows a level of sensitivity in establishing
academic goals and helping students work towards them. 'Establishing academic goals' is hard work if a person has become overwhelmed by family
or social definitions of study, and a study counsellor's role is to help students hear their own internal voices, and start the slow journey towards
valuing their own internal standards. There are two extreme attitudes which

arise out of conflicts around 'internal standards' and cause people problems with assessed academic work, especially writing. One is having so little sense of one's own academic values that self-esteem comes entirely from other people's judgements; and the other is having such over-the-top internal values that it becomes impossible ever to complete anything, as no work is ever perfect enough. A combination also happens, where over-the-top perfectionism is ascribed to externals, such as tutors, markers and fellow students, because there is not enough confidence to claim those perfectionist standards personally.

We all need others' approval and affirmation to an extent. For those who have not yet developed personal, internal standards there is little more painful than having one's work marked. Where the need for approval is deep, unconstructively learnt or the outcome of relationships with adults who are inappropriately invasive, mentally or physically, the engagement with academic exercises can be highly stressful. For it re-enacts, formally, the process of presenting yourself, via work, for the approval of others. Where there are no internal standards, or they are excessively perfectionist, then the assessment procedure will be experienced as devastating. Depending entirely on outside appraisal for a sense of worth is designed to bring feelings of agitation and distress, especially when, after unhappy experiences, academic tasks have become associated with bad feelings. Hewitt (1992: 176), when summarizing modes of relaxation, has written that it is mistaken 'to base self-worth on competitive performance standards', for the habit of comparing oneself with others in occupation, status, appearance or possessions is one effective way of increasing stress and worry. This does not mean that all competition is unhealthy, nor does it negate the ego-boost earned by praise from a respected source or the thrill of completing a task well. Rather, it means that the whole of one's self-worth should not lie in the hands of others' judgements and by comparison with others' failures.

The notion that anything which is less than perfect is going to subject the student to public humiliation, exposure as a fraud, hilarity of tutors and fellow students and general opprobrium is a common enough feeling. For many, university has been a place for clever people, which, by definition, has not included them, hence they ascribe to university work a standard well in advance of what is actually required to pass courses. Just passing is rarely enough, and, albeit unwittingly, better-than-average marks can be used as a justification for taking up what seems like a precious place, especially to mature students. The underlying assumption is that the place really belongs by rights to someone else, who could make better use of it. It can be hard for friends and tutors to accept that someone getting first-class and upper-second marks is trying to say there is a backlog because that person does not feel capable or entitled to do the degree. It is equally as hard for students to hear and accept that they are not the first to feel like this, nor will they be the last, and that others actually do understand these strenuously hidden feelings.

The academic starting point for tackling the issue of 'internal standards' is working to help students express their view of an assignment (as suggested in Chapters 5 and 6). This then becomes the basis by which one makes sense of complex, new material: whatever the topic, the first step is to find out students' own responses, opinions and existing knowledge, before going near textbooks. Science students assume this approach does not include them; however, establishing one's existing understanding of a topic is a helpful first step to ironing out misunderstandings. By unravelling what one thinks already, reading can be approached with a series of questions in mind, with an enquiring interest rather than a dispirited expectation that it will all be difficult and impenetrable. The assumption that science is entirely factual, never changes and is not a subject about which one has opinions or preferences is, of itself, a rewarding area for examination when trying to unravel what study means to individual students.

Valuing personal style

Helping people improve how they study is about encouraging students to develop their own style of working and to learn to be confident about it. Adjusting new study techniques to suit existing ways of working is usually more successful than trying to become a different person or to imitate others' styles. Obviously this requires students to describe what it is they do already, how and when they study, but lack of respect for their own work habits makes this difficult for them to do and can involve the study counsellor or tutor in asking questions. Additionally, asking how people spend their time can make the counsellor appear highly critical of students' time management habits, so caution is required in asking apparently innocuous questions.

Time management can be about matching the time available to the tasks to be done. Another, less mechanistic, approach is to get to know yourself better, learning when you do certain jobs best and what you experience as rewarding activity. This way one hopes to enjoy life a little more, introduce variety and a sense of achievement, rather than living as if all that matters is meeting a series of deadlines. One way of avoiding asking invasive questions is to write a 'personal study inventory' which students can use privately if using them face-to-face seems too daunting. Inventories are not usual ways of going about counselling meetings, so giving out personal study questionnaires to students to take away can be a helpful means of setting 'homework', allowing people time to reflect during the week on how they go about study. Students do not have to report back their findings to a counsellor or tutor if they do not wish, but can use their answers as a private means of exploring their own study preferences and start learning to take these preferences seriously.

One kind of question to be explored is at what time of day the student works best. Most of us have to work at times which do not suit us well, and find some jobs are easier to do in the morning and others easier to do at other times. These combinations are worth discussing because out of the variations comes a sense of personal preference in tandem with increased awareness of the demands of particular tasks. Likewise the question where the student works best? Not only does this depend on the time available, the season (winter and heating expenses), and the job to be done, but such a simple question can begin to unravel the severe impact on academic work of being unhappily housed. Problems with lighting, problems with flatmates: some accommodation problems can be tackled, while others have to be tolerated.

Preferences cannot always be implemented, one cannot be in control of all aspects of life, however important, such as whether one prefers to work in silence or with background noise? Noisy halls of residence and inconsiderate housemates can wind people up to excessive levels of tension, cause sleepless nights and so add new layers to problems. Mediation between warring neighbours may not seem an obvious part of the jobs of tutor or counsellor and, indeed, it is a role which might be better carried out by others (such as student union representatives, accommodation office officials or halls of residence managers), but occasional practical interventions can help.

What are students' preferred patterns of working: every weekday night; very hard some nights, leaving others free; always having weekends free; using weekends to catch up with missed work; only working during the day, never at night? In asking this question one asks, indirectly, what it is that stops people following their preferred courses of action. There are 'constraints' which cannot be negotiated, such as lecture or seminar times. Other constraints may require further discussion: the inability to say 'no' when friends knock on the door or make offers of coffee. Learning to be assertive may not be enough on its own if there is an underlying fear that one will not have friends if a refusal is ever given.

In spite of the universality of deadlines in academic life, students react quite differently to assignments. This is revealed by asking them how they respond to deadlines. Some start at once, others wait until they have talked to fellow students or heard the lecture; some wait until near the deadline and rush it in on time, others always hand in their work after the deadline. The notion that there are choices in how one responds to a deadline is a liberating one for people who find the imposition of dates claustrophobic. Personal responses to deadlines do reveal levels of grievance with tutors' lack of personal interest in students' progress, and uncover confusion that no one cares if work is not completed and tutors do not chase individual students to find out why they have not completed work.

The process, then, of defining a personal style of study is time-consuming and detailed. It may underpin a number of meetings, building up a personal study portrait while apparently 'meandering' into the byways which emerge. Some byways may lead to practical plans for students to alter or amend their situations, when possible, so that life becomes more conducive to study. Other byways may just be made easier to navigate because they have been discussed openly. The main journey remains one which takes students nearer to understanding their own styles of study.

Valuing ideas

Mills (1959: 196) described scholarship as 'a choice of how to live as well as a choice of career', and goes on to offer a personal account of how he went about his craft. Central to his craft of becoming a social scientist is the practice of keeping notes of thoughts and experiences, so developing 'self-reflective habits' from which 'you learn how to keep your inner world awake' (1959: 197). This has a practical byproduct, as Mills suggests, of ensuring regular practice in writing. Students usually only write about academic matters when they are to be assessed, so rarely experience the liberating effects of exploring their own ideas in combination with the written word. Exercise 7.1 is designed to help people build confidence in the value of their own ideas, and to provide a means for learning to 'write badly'. It is a formalized version of Mills's 'file', which is the academic equivalent of keeping a diary.

Exercise 7.1: Keeping an academic diary

For five minutes *only*, and ten minutes if you are a postgraduate, jot down any ideas that have occurred to you during the day. It might just be a question or a series of questions which occurred to you during a lecture, a seminar or while reading. It does not matter how embryonic or sketchy the ideas are. It helps to use a notepad especially for these ideas.

Take half an hour every two weeks to look back at the contents of the notepad and ask some questions:

• Can I remember why that seemed important then?
• What do I want to add to each set of writings?
• Are there any obvious themes running through my ideas?
• Are some topics/lectures/subjects/media triggering ideas more often than others?

Ideally this exercise should be carried out in a conducive environment, with pleasant music or a good view. If these criteria are not possible, at the very least, there should be no screaming children, partners, flatmates, mayhem and mess about. The exercises are kept short deliberately to make it easier to arrange 'uninterruptable' sessions.

People with word-processors can edit in the answers to these questions. Postgraduates should be more systematic in doing this, perhaps allowing an hour at the end of every week for editing in developments, or adding shopping-lists of questions that need to be followed up, relevant books to read, directions that need developing. Anyone who is involved in writing journal articles, or thinks that they ought to be, will find this a useful (albeit slow) way to start, especially if they are already laden with teaching and administration.

Academic study is part of a person's whole life. How they feel about the world, themselves and their prior experience is intimately woven into the academic problems faced. While it is not the study counsellor's role to challenge students with these deeper echoes, it is a part of the role to be conscious of and sensitive to these undercurrents, and to work with an awareness of them. The counsellor's openness to these matters means that students feel freer in discussing the more painful aspects of life and should receive acceptance and understanding. The study counsellor's aim is to open up the student's ability to hear their own inner voice, value their own thoughts and insights, and depend less destructively on external assessments. Outside valuations, however, are always unnerving for most of us, and extremely disturbing to some, triggering and creating extremes of fear. In the next chapter I look at two aspects of academic life which cause high levels of fear: one is anything to do with numbers; and the other is the formal examination. Both of these can trigger all the elements discussed in this chapter, and a few more besides.

8

Fear: Numbers and Examinations

Two areas of academic life are particularly capable of inducing fear: numerical work and sitting examinations. The continuum of fear stretches from mild frissons of dislike through anxiety to abject terror. I use the words 'fear' and 'anxiety' interchangeably. Fear is considered to be a reasonable response in the face of a life-threatening danger or extremely unpleasant event, such as meeting a lion in the kitchen or the anticipation of torture. Like fear, anxiety is a series of unpleasant sensations, both physical and mental, which stimulate and are part of the 'fight or flight' response to a perceived danger. The difference, traditionally, is that with 'anxiety' others do not recognize the stimulus as appropriate to the response – for example, regularly avoiding going into the kitchen due a dread of meeting a lion in there. Anxiety is a problem when it becomes crippling. So people who were taught arithmetic by the well-known method of knocking children off their chairs and across rooms have learnt a fear response – after all, an out-of-control adult suddenly attacking a five-year-old must be experienced as life-threatening. (I do not know why this method was so popular, but I have heard it so many times now that I feel it must have been a recommended teaching technique in the 1950s.) The fear response in the adult becomes anxiety: it is a misplaced fear in an adult who is not in danger and it cripples that person's choices about learning.

Learning arithmetic and mathematics requires a logical progression, and if anything gets in the way of that it becomes harder and harder for children to progress. Any elements missed in the early days stretch a long shadow over people's lives, encouraging a belief in their innumeracy which limits chances and options in life to a startling extent. If mathematics was taught violently or became associated with severe anxiety in the early days, then the adult suffers the same anxiety years later and finds they are still 'unable' to learn anything numerical; strong emotions can erupt unexpectedly, to the surprise of all concerned (Peelo 1994). Some mature students have overcome these fears to a certain extent, but find their ability to progress on courses which include numerical work of any kind severely inhibited. Adults add to past failures the new embarrassment of panic experienced in lecture theatres – while no one else may have noticed, they have re-experienced the panicky child, but this time in a public lecture theatre.

Many responses hide under the umbrella term 'examination anxiety', but students' experiences and situations are different. One person may find examinations uncomfortable, others may have experienced failure which they dread repeating, and yet more are just lacking confidence in the face of academic challenges. Dyslexic students can become tense under the pressure of time, and worry well in advance of examination that their handwriting will be illegible. One student may have experienced panic in an examination many months before, and have become increasingly tense, tired and panicky, carrying a secret terror of a repeat performance. The panic can become so great that even going near the original examination hall sparks echoes of a panic attack. For sufferers of depression or students slipping into a generalized state of anxiety, examinations add to the discomfort, especially if they are also facing huge 'life decisions' about future work, graduation or partnerships.

Numbers

On rare occasions tutor/counsellors meet students who are phobic about anything numeric. They choose courses which are manifestly unquantitative, and seek help because they cannot read government statistics, get to grips with information presented in tabular form or, indeed, understand any quantitative material, and a project demands skills such as these. The systematic teaching required to fill in the gaps of a lifetime, step-by-step at the student's pace, with a frightened adult, is probably best done on a programme designed for people in a similar situation and properly resourced with the staff, equipment and materials needed for the enterprise. A study counsellor can offer support while students go through such numeracy programmes, discussing the fears raised and the anxieties stirred up, but cannot provide the actual teaching required. I have, in the past, helped students plan how they will go about finding courses and programmes of study, once a lot of time has been spent discussing doubts, fears and frustrations, and setting up a series of 'numeracy' goals towards which they would like to work over time. The amount of time to be allocated to this depends on: how terrified a student is; what programmes are available locally; and how pressing the need is to master basic skills.

The terror felt by non-numerate students can be mixed up with issues of 'good taste': the 'positivist' debates within some disciplines (especially in the social sciences) makes it easier to disdain numbers as inherently bad symbols of themselves, thus avoiding engagement with a feared area of work. The 'positivist' debate is essential in making students aware of the philosophies underlying the choice of research methods in their chosen fields of study, but the tools used by positivists to substantiate their analyses and beliefs are a strange way to justify terror. Once you have the appropriate knowledge and understanding, you may *choose* to cut yourself off from a system of communication, but for those who cannot cope with the tools of the trade then there are no real choices. Education, if it has any purposes at all, must help people to widen their choices about how they think, and not perpetuate prejudice by closing down entry to alternative systems of thought.

More usually, tutor/counsellors meet students on science courses or courses with high numeracy requirements in order to understand material. Particularly among mature students returning later in life, severe anxiety is stirred up at the points where their understanding falters. However much they may have learnt in a lifetime and may perceive themselves to have coped, the anxiety with which they are flooded when faced with a numerical challenge comes as a rude shock. Like non-numerate students, they experience a sheer physical sense of walking into a brick wall of incomprehension when sitting in lectures, so much so that some believe that there is something physically wrong with their brain which makes them incapable of advancing mathematically.

Mathematics taught as a series of instructions to anxious adults merely reinforces the anxiety and failure; what is required is a change of mindset, a different way of looking at things. To achieve this is difficult for counsellors and teachers, because the anxiety makes adult learners cling to the known, and insist on being 'tutored'. Students will assume that as a counsellor you have never met anyone before with this problem, and that counselling has nothing to offer. On occasion I meet this problem under instructions from the student: there's nothing you can do, but I want tutoring arranged for me. These factors can make it extremely difficult to set up a relationship in which there is a sense of trust because:

- by now the backlog is huge;
- the backlog on other courses has grown because the amount of time taken to keep up with mathematical elements is out of all proportion to the quantity of numerical work required;
- people assume that they alone have ever faced this problem;
- even if people know that others face this problem, then they believe that no one else panics to the same extent as they do;
- it will be assumed, more often than not, that 'caring' is not scientific, so you will know nothing about these problems.

Similar to the positivist debate with non-numerate students, an inflexible view of what science is and should be is a part of the problem. The beliefs that science is 'hard' and unemotional, that it is factually fixed and understood only by the few initiates make it harder for such students to seek and to receive help. Anyone teaching 'remedial' mathematics classes for science students would be well advised to seek help with course design so that they can take account of the students' needs, rather than just trying speedily to 'plug' gaps in knowledge. While trying to reach someone gripped by anxiety and worry as they learn to live with panic and not fear it and offering solace as daydreams about gaining degrees begin to fade, a study counsellor needs to ensure that students are also beginning to unravel the impact of poor early teaching on their later capacity to learn. This is a tall order, and might come after some practical suggestions.

Adjectives, quantities and relationships

Science students usually describe their basic education as 'good', and while this is probably so, one cannot take this statement at face value, for the anxiety and lack of confidence they experience with numbers has to have come from somewhere. Whereas non-numerate students know that their mathematical education was unsuccessful. People believe that they were 'well taught' if they experienced highly disciplined classrooms and rote learning, especially with arithmetic. But, as we saw was indicated with reading (see Chapter 5), good teaching sows the seeds which make it possible for pupils to take the next learning step. Recitation and familiarity provide a firm foundation for arithmetic. There is no easier start than knowing your 'times tables', except that it can be boring and children can produce appropriate-sounding noises which have no meaning. In addition, for many people taught before the early 1960s, violence was used in recitation exercises, operating rather like electric shocks might in 'aversion therapy'. However, familiarity and recitation are not sufficient foundations of themselves to enable children to move on to develop mathematical skills. For numbers are not only adjectives or quantities as we teach children ('one' duck, 'two' ducks), they are in fact shorthand notations which summarize relationships (this is a much bigger debate than can be dealt with by me; see, for example, Russell 1967). Speaking crudely, a numerical relationship means we only understand one because we know about two, and one has a specific relationship/ratio to two.

To develop mathematically, children need a more abstract understanding of the philosophy of number, albeit in a pragmatic, applied way. Students may have learnt about neatness and obedience in laying out a sum properly on the page, but they should also have learnt about the changing values of numbers according to where they are 'placed'. A child can remember that noughts make numbers bigger by ten without any sense of what this means, so still 'perform' well in tests. Children might have been told that noughts increase the value of a number by ten, and that where a number is placed increases its value also, yet to complete a sum a teacher might have said: 'To add 215 to 310: nought plus five is five; one plus one is two; two plus three is five. That makes 525.' Logically the teacher's words meant: 'nought plus five is five; ten plus ten is 20; 200 plus 300 is 500. That makes 525.' It feels quite different to the child who has not understood complex numerical relationships, yet adults say it is the same thing to call 500 'five', just quicker.

Remember that children learn to count by using numbers as adjectives, describing an actual quantifiable piece of matter. As a quantity, 500 ducks is a totally different matter to five ducks. Calling 500 'five' makes sense because we have done so many times, but calling 500 'five' is, in effect, a transformation similar to the function of logarithms, where very large numbers are called something else quite specific, based on the relationship between log and original number. That is, it is not accidental that 500 is called 'five', rather than 'four' or 'two', because five is in a quite specific relationship with 500 according to the shorthand (symbolism) of where it is placed. It is not unknown for almost the identical sensations felt by the non-comprehending child to reappear in the adult who is struggling with transformation of quantities. Anxiety can escalate if, for example, that person has accommodated anxiety by developing a preference for applied measurement techniques in research, for example, and transformation of quantities emerges as an important laboratory skill.

The combination of this sort of misdirected thinking or confusion with general unhappiness can be a disastrous recipe for a child. Along with misdirected thinking and confusion goes the too-easy acceptance of low standards from some children, especially those from 'bad' homes. People who have experienced 'good teaching' may have learnt well what they were taught, but be unaware of what was missed out or why. Robert Roberts (1976: 156) describes how, at school, he was told that the headteacher did not enter pupils for a public examination because they had to know algebra and geometry, 'Well above anything we do'. Women on science courses may not be aware when assumptions are being made about knowledge gleaned not from the National Curriculum but from a lifetime of boyish pursuits – mending cars, bicycles, television sets and so forth. By definition, we do not know what was missed out, taught badly, or seen as beyond our abilities, so gaps can exist for even the best-taught. That is what the adult brings to undergraduate work: an acceptance of others' estimations of stupidity coupled with unexpected, frightening anxiety, possibly built on an insecure sense of what numbers are about.

Practical suggestions

The following suggestions do not constitute miracles, but provide practical steps for nervous science students to take when facing problems with numerical work. These steps are dependent on the students having experienced some prior success with numerical work, even if there are gaps in their education. As with all study techniques, there is much trial and error in trying to find strategies to suit particular individuals and their courses of study.

Lists
To break down the sense of all numerical work being difficult, student and study counsellor compile a detailed list of what numerical skills,

computational and mathematical, the student needs to master to complete the course both to the university standard and to the student's own standard. The list, initially, may be retrospective, combing through last term's work for an accurate account of what needs to be understood, rather than an anxiety-laden anticipation of what *may* need to be done to get through what is coming during the following terms.

In individual sessions we will talk about the list. Again, the intention is to move away from a generalized expression of discomfort, to a specific discussion of the student's response to each item on the list. This includes: why the topic is likeable, loathable, difficult, easy; when the topic was first met (nine times out of ten there is no memory of this, usually because it was not taught at an earlier stage); and what emotions were experienced when the topic was introduced (for the first time as well as more recently).

Explanation sheets

As with earlier 'summary sheets' (see Chapter 5), these are sheets of paper laid out in a set form, for students to fill in. Having a pretyped form obliges the form-filler to be tidy, to take the work more seriously, and implies filing completed work. The form starts with date, course and topic. These simple pieces of information place complex material in a context which, while intellectually meaningless in some senses, does not depend only on understanding for some rudimentary recall (at this point we are not necessarily talking about ideal forms of learning).

The next item on the sheet is a square, allowing about six lines of writing: this square is called 'purpose' (or whatever word seems most relevant to the student's course). The object of this exercise is to encourage students to ask *why* a given aspect of mathematical work appeared at a particular point in the course, and what its general use is, such as measurement of specific sorts of laboratory activity. This often begs questions about traditional modes of research, intentions in using statistics or analysing results, all of which are relevant responses to academic endeavour which should be recorded as questions. These questions are the bases for understanding and memory whether or not the student has answers, and what matters is that they begin to engage with their adult responses to learning.

The remaining space on the page is taken up with recording any essential procedures. This might be a formula (even if this is a combination of steps derived from a variety of mathematical sources), it might be the steps taken when using a calculator to find logarithms. The second side of the page is to be used for notes of any personal research into the topic (see 'Research'). The explanation sheet should be filed in front of notes taken from lectures, seminars or wherever formal teaching of the topic has occurred.

Research

Students do not have much time to spare, especially science students whose weeks are timetabled away in long practical sessions. The chances of carrying out personal research when panicky are limited. The research envisaged here is, in fact, a search: through children's bookshops, student bookshops and libraries looking for the easiest possible explanation of the topic in question. A 'Noddy and Big Ears' account of a skill or a concept can provide a basic framework, on to which can be grafted more sophisticated understanding. One inspired example of this reported to me was a departmental manager handing out children's books on how computers work to staff whose office was about to be computerized. It is these lower-level explanations which should be noted on the back of 'explanation sheets', in advance of the complex ones presented in lectures. The framework may, in the end, be too simple, but once some understanding is established, then simplicity can be replaced with a more sophisticated approach.

Verbal explanations
Having to explain to someone who is more frightened or who knows less than you do is a highly effective method of coming to understand your subject better. Explaining a topic to the study counsellor is one means of achieving this. A longer-term strategy is to enrol as a tutor for adults with numeracy problems, including fear, or to involve oneself with teaching mathematics and arithmetic. I have often toyed with the notion of introducing number-phobic students to science students with these difficulties.

Self-help groups
A variation on 'verbal explanations' is for groups of students with similar difficulties to work together. Unfortunately, most feel they are, as individuals, particularly stupid, and avoid detailed or open discussion. But, for example, if 'remedial' classes are a part of a science course, then it is easier for a group to approach, together, a department and request assistance in setting up a group (such as a room in which to meet, extra problem sheets).

Timetables
Two timetables need to be established for private numerical work: one is for getting through the present year of the course (which includes allowing time to catch up with backlogs), and the other is for getting through the degree. Life can become less pressured if these two timetables are separated, and vacations can be used to 'buy time' to achieve longer-term learning goals. Establishing these two timetables may require advice from a sympathetic tutor, who is prepared to sit down and work out what is possible, what is essential and what is optional. Once it is decided which tasks belong to which timetable, then one can work on devising strategies to achieve these learning goals.

Underlying all of these practical suggestions is a desire for perfection, shared by many students across all courses at university. It can be disappointing for students to be told that they should not expect 100 per cent success on science courses, and some take this as a personal assessment of their capabilities (or lack of them). Learning to let go and be satisfied with less than perfection is part of a wider approach to life which cannot be answered by study techniques. It is, of course, one of the most valuable lessons to be learnt when it comes to sitting examinations.

Examinations

Although excellent alternative assessment procedures to the traditional examination are available (see, for example, Andresen *et al.* 1993; and Gibbs *et al.* 1988), it is still the case that every summer hundreds of thousands of students traipse into hangar-like halls to be examined. Not all students hate examinations, but the stress involved can be great, and for some they are utter misery. Anxiety is worsened by knowing that you might have been able to do better, for only if you are in danger of doing well is there much to fear or to lose. A part of anxiety is the feeling that examinations are events that happen to you, like floods or earthquakes, over which you have no control: you do not know what the questions are going to be; you do not know what the standard is; and there is the uncomfortable feeling that you do not understand what is expected. Examination anxiety can be lessened a little by learning to recognize what actually happens in university examinations; and even students who hate examinations can act to ensure that what positive, personal advantages there are in sitting examinations are timetabled into revision.

Preparing for revision

One of the myths about studying for a degree is that everyone hates examinations. This is not true: some people prefer them to coursework assessment and enjoy the challenge, while other people are neutral about exams. Many people have mixed feelings, enjoying parts and hating other bits. It is hard to work out how you feel about examinations if everyone around you is complaining about how worried they are. So one of the first jobs in individual sessions with students is to track down exactly what their personal mixture of feelings is, including their likes as well as dislikes; what advantages they can see in doing examinations; and setting up revision timetables which fit individual needs as well as course requirements.

The technique of 'reviewing' (see Chapter 4) is helpful at examination time, allowing students to look back at the academic year and see what they still wish to achieve. Revision time can be used to review the year. Was it fun? Was it misery? Reviewing the year constructively develops the use of highly personal responses to academic work as aids to memory and recall. Some ideas to think about together:

> What do you think of the subject matter, now that you know more?
> What was the teaching style like: Interesting? Entertaining? Did you
>   just cover the basics or add to what you have learnt elsewhere?

Knowing what you know now, would you choose that subject again?
Given this year's experience, what subjects do you think you'll choose
  next year, and why?

It sounds unlikely, I know, to suggest that one considers the advantages of
doing examinations when talking to nervous students. But most human
beings experience mixed motives about their activities, so it should not be
too surprising to hear that even quite frightened undergraduates recognize
personal advantages in examinations. The underlying question is: 'Since I
have to do examinations, what do I want out of the experience?' Some commonly heard 'advantages' of sitting examinations:

- Rounding off the year – pulling the strands together.
- Finding out what topics have been enjoyed and understood.
- The 'impersonal' setting – some people enjoy this.
- Exams are time-limited exercises – unlike coursework, they can be done
  and left behind.

Before rushing on to working out a daily revision timetable on the basis
of what course material has to be covered in the time available, people
need to decide what they are trying to achieve when revising: are they trying
to read through all their existing notes in the hope that something will stick
to the brain, or are they going to prepare for an examination? Preparing
means:

- striving for understanding – where there is understanding, then memory
  follows more easily;
- mentally rehearsing what actually happens in the examination;
- ensuring that there is variety (to avoid boredom and staleness), flexibility
  and realism about what is possible.

Preparation is also researching the examination itself: past papers, seminar
groups, lectures and mock examinations are all means of investigating the
structure of the test to be taken. If the examination requires essay-style answers then memorizing all the course notes is not enough, whereas learning
three topics in depth will not do for a multiple-choice test. These differences should be reflected in a revision timetable.

Revision

The study counsellor needs to be clear about what a particular student finds
difficult about revision, although this can get lost under general assumptions about how problematic examinations can be (besides, it might not be
the actual event that the student fears, just the run-up).

What do you find most difficult about revising?
How do you usually deal with that?

Students' usual approaches to revision are often being jettisoned when they approach staff for help, either because the methods used have already shown themselves to be inadequate (by marks earned in other examinations) or because students have, for some reason, lost confidence in their usual approach. One step, then, in helping students to revise is to find out what it is they do already:

How do you usually go about revision?
How have you been intending to revise this time?
Is this different to what you usually do?
What made you change?

When discussing personal revision styles people are sometimes too nervous to be clear what this might mean, yet what they are doing already is often perfectly adequate for the style of examination. Tutor/counsellors can find themselves offering reassurance, convincing students that other people's styles of working may not be right for their subjects or temperament, even though they can pick up useful hints from friends and colleagues. Finding out how people revise should be more than a generalized chat about usual practices; it should be a way of defining closely what a student's approach to learning is, why learning is approached that way, and why changes are being made. It is also a time for students to consider alternative techniques to absorb into their usual approaches. If there is not an opportunity in individual sessions, a handout can be designed including questions about usual study methods:

Do you ever:
• Revise with friends?
• Attend revision seminars?
• Look at past examination papers in your subjects?
• Decide whether to use only your notes or go and find other relevant material?
• Do test questions?
• Make summaries of your notes?
• Test yourself on what you have learnt?
• Allow more time for topics you do not understand?
• Make a list of topics you have liked during the year?
• Make a list of topics you have hated?
• Study related topics at the same time?
• Decide your working hours?
• Have time for leisure?
• Allow for variety in your timetable?

Describing how one revises is not, immediately, as informative as it sounds: people can be engaged in quite different activities, for example, when they say 'I just go through my notes'. What students perceive learning to be about is an integral part of how they approach revision and what they expect to do when revising. One famous division of learning is into 'deep' and 'surface' approaches (Marton *et al.* 1984): in general terms, a 'deep' approach is one which values concepts, understanding and making connections between ideas or information; whereas 'surface' learning is typified by expectations of memorizing individual facts without a context of understanding. Most revision styles should combine these approaches, according to the purpose in learning and the style of examination to be taken. Students who concentrate on memory and view examinations as an opportunity to 'dump' knowledge which will not be needed afterwards are likely to find being examined highly stressful, and will worry about the reliability of their memory. 'Going through notes' will, in all probability, be a 'passive' reading in the hopes of memorizing lecture notes. Students with a more holistic approach to learning are likely to have accumulated a sounder understanding of their courses throughout the year, so revision builds on what has gone before. Their notes are more likely to be grounded in earlier understanding, from essays, projects, laboratory reports as well as lectures, and revision can, therefore, turn into an active, questioning exercise.

Preparing to sit examinations

Students do not always realize that they can make certain choices about mentally preparing themselves close to the examination. They may have spent years being wound up before examinations by chattering friends without becoming aware that this makes it worse. Asking the question 'How do you prefer to wait?' can release people to take on a different style, one which feels slightly more in control of events. Tutor/counsellors can help students design how they would prefer to wait before going into the examination if this seems helpful. The issues to be discussed include:

1. Do you like to wait with other people?
2. Do you prefer your own company?
3. Do you like a period of quiet?
4. Do you prefer to arrive early and wait nearby?
5. Do you like to have a walk, swim, etc. first?
6. Do you feel better if you have sorted out pencils, pens, etc. the night before?
7. How do you feel about eating before an examination?
8. Do you become more uncomfortable reading notes at the last minute?
9. Do you become more uncomfortable being parted from your notes?

Waiting for an afternoon examination means there is a lot of 'hanging around' time – how does the student like to spend that time and is it the best way? What has made matters worse in the past, and what can be done to avoid previous pitfalls? It is easy to say 'relax', but a few relaxation techniques learnt and practised in advance can come in particularly useful if an examination starts later in the day.

I have in the past used Exercise 8.1 with students as a 'warm-up' exercise in examination workshops, but it is interesting for staff to try as well. It brings out into the open some of the simplest and most basic assumptions about taking examinations, which get buried under a welter of worry.

Exercise 8.1: Preparing for examinations

Discuss how important you think the following are when sitting an exam.

- Timing – equal allocation of time per question.
- Checking if there are compulsory questions.
- Reading the instructions at the top of the exam paper.
- Bringing the right equipment.
- Revising up to the last possible second.
- Doing the correct number of questions.
- Turning up to the exam after everyone else has gone in and started.
- Allowing enough time to check through your answers.
- Clarity in setting out figures in mathematical exercises.
- Looking up the location of the exam room just before the exam starts.
- Clear handwriting.
- Start writing as soon as you see a question you can answer.

Questions about what kind of examination, what sort of learning, students are working towards should have been discussed in early sessions with a tutor/counsellor. Long before the actual day itself students will have found out, with the study counsellor's encouragement, the length and style of an examination, its location and what equipment they need to take. Another element of 'thinking oneself' into the examination is to test oneself: knowledge is more easily recalled if we apply it instead of trying to recall information in a vacuum, but this does not mean sitting down and writing out full answers to every question on past papers. 'Testing' can be done by applying knowledge to old questions, doing quick outlines of answers and roughing out how one arrives at solutions.

Testing is an ideal time for developing strategies, based on understanding material, for ways of coping in the examination if there appears to be nothing in one's memory bank relevant to the question. The approach to adopt is one of expecting to work for three hours: this means actively cudgelling the brain rather than just waiting for information to spill out. With essay-type answers, a common approach is to 'rough out' an answer after quickly jotting down what is to be included. Dealing with questions of which you know little is just an extension of this method coupled with a small amount of lateral thinking. The following group exercise describes this strategy:

Exercise 8.2: Working in the examination

In groups, pool your imaginations and see how you might try to answer the following question (groups can be given different questions):

Compare and contrast the outbreak of civil unrest which occurred among horse owners in the 1920s and cattle breeders of the same period.

Discuss the incidence of ginger cats in Great Britain in the nineteenth century.

'The popularity of Australian soap operas in recent years reflects a need to escape from dreary alienation and recession' (Bloggs). Critically analyse this view of television as a social tranquillizer.

This exercise can require tutors to work with groups to get them to understand that one can use the imagination to conjure up an answer, and these questions concentrate minds on the process involved rather than the knowledge needed. So, a group might start to discuss horse breeders:

Who are they? Where did they live? Surely it depends what course you're doing what they want from you? Maybe there were high taxes? Maybe they were violent people – particular people? The bottom had fallen out of the horse-buying market – changes in transport – government subsidy of transport?

What starts as a group game, with no one knowing anything about the subject, ends with a list of questions about an imaginary event, all of which can form the core of an answer. Allowing equal time per examination question leaves time for this kind of thinking. Integrating this form of 'testing' into revision itself encourages practice of a strategy to use when one's mind 'blanks' or little is known about the topic, and is a more fun way to encourage recall of what has been revised.

Living with fear: long-term

None of the study strategies mentioned already will prevent panic or change students into non-anxious people, although they may make life more comfortable and enable revision to occur. The truth about panic and anxiety is that, in the long-term, the only ways to live with them both include exposure to the objects or situations which trigger these responses (preferably with support), coupled with applying oneself to learning how to live in a more relaxed way. This is not welcome news to anyone who is panicking, because it takes a long time to show any benefits.

A simple starting point is to introduce some rewards or pampering into life. Drawing up a list of items a student might look forward to is difficult for the depressed and highly anxious to do when they have little sense of pleasure or worthiness. A 'reward' list needs to be cheap, and must not include unhealthy addictions. The deeper fear, that one is not worthy of love, attention, pampering or reward, needs to be thought about, perhaps with a sympathetic counsellor. The aim is to get off the punishing treadmill of a grey, grim and harassed life.

Some of the traditional longer-term strategies are meditation and relaxation techniques coupled with improved physical fitness. These techniques can be learnt by buying commercial tapes, books, videos or attending classes (although the latter is difficult for people who are finding life a struggle). The benefits of increased relaxation over time are hard to quantify but they include: increased capacity to cope with panic, greater confidence, sense of ease, replenishing sleep, less damage to spine and general enjoyment of everyday events. At the end of the day, students who study in their bedrooms move from books to bed with no hope of sleeping. All the working stimuli need to be removed, and work should stop in time to wind down – easy to say but harder to do. In the longer term it helps if students can recover their interests outside academic study, even if this only stretches to watching television. Some variation in the pace of life to offset the intensity of academic worries is soothing, but tends to come more easily only as people feel fairly relaxed and confident. To relax, people must leave behind the punitive attitude which says 'I cannot go out, I have not done well enough', and learn instead to take breaks and join in with other activities.

Underneath it all is a fear of letting go, a resistance to relaxing, the belief that your anxiety is different. Anxiety inhibits what students feel able to join in at university and the underlying belief that they are not good enough constrains people, as they battle to avoid being 'found out' as frauds. It is this thinking which makes workshops, which I look at in the next chapter, a difficult form of teaching, as students experience intense and personal feelings in a public forum.

9

Workshops

Anyone who engages in study work is likely to become involved in running sessions for large numbers of students on some aspect of what is usually called 'study skills'. Teaching study skills goes against the grain of one-to-one work, which responds to individual needs, and can reinforce the view that study is reducible to a series of techniques. The favoured method, then, of teaching 'study' in a manner which offsets a mechanistic impression is the workshop, which is based on the assumption that students' own experiences are relevant to learning. A study workshop concentrates on students actively learning rather than teaching decontextualized study techniques through teachers' individual performances. Workshops can be fun and exciting for participants and facilitators, but they can also be miserable and frightening experiences for both. Workshop-style teaching methods are currently popular because they appear to hold answers to how one processes large numbers of students through courses without substantially increasing staff numbers. There can, however, be a degree of naivety about what can go wrong and what can go well, and it helps to consider some ground rules in advance and talk to people experienced in workshops – both as participants and organizers.

Employers will, rightly, expect study counsellors to be capable of engaging in preventive work by teaching students from across all departments in a university about study and study techniques. This does not mean relapsing into a teaching mode which offers hopelessly generalized titbits of advice; rather, it means developing materials and methods which enable students to use their existing personal resources while testing out new ideas and methods. This assumes a student-centred approach which enables participants to reflect positively and constructively on what they do already, without putting individual students in a position where they must confess personal detail to strangers.

Experiential teaching and learning

The phrase 'experiential learning' currently holds a number of meanings: one refers to the translation of prior experience into units which can be recognized and accredited by an institution; and another refers to learning through the experience of taking part in a particular activity, such as laboratory work, sandwich course work experience, and workshop exercises (for a fuller discussion of these two meanings, see Evans 1992).

Both these meanings imply a third, which is an underlying philosophy of what constitutes learning. That philosophy refers to the belief that learning is a lifelong process of adaptation – as Kolb (1993: 150) put it: 'learning involves transactions between the person and the environment'. 'Experiential learning' is primarily an integrative theory, for by accepting learning as holistic one acknowledges that it can occur wherever reflective human beings live and breathe, instead of decontextualizing learning in a mechanistic model. Evans (1992: 136) describes the process of accrediting prior university experience as one which requires students to reflect upon their experience and to be able to show what they have learned from it, which can be seen as a practical, specific, example of what Kolb (1993: 153) means when he talks about learning being the process of creating knowledge:

> Knowledge is the result of the transaction between social knowledge and personal knowledge. The former, as Dewey noted, is the civilized objective accumulation of previous human cultural experience, whereas the latter is the accumulation of the individual person's subjective life experiences. Knowledge results from the transaction between these objective and subjective experiences in a process called learning.

Study workshops concentrate on encouraging students to understand that their subjective experience can be trusted, and that the personal experience and knowledge of their fellow students is also relevant to negotiating a degree course. Kolb's view is, of course, more than Evans's accreditation, because Kolb is describing a combination of public and private knowledge; what surprises many students in study workshops is that they expect an exposition of the social accumulation of knowledge (the expert's guide on how to study) and cannot see what their own experience has to do with learning. The lessons of other people's experience and educationists' theories can be usefully applied to one's own life only when mediated through personal knowledge, and not used as a replacement.

A major barrier to students' active participation in workshops is anxiety. Adults are filled with terror at the prospect of displaying their stupidity in front of others and of making fools of themselves. No matter how kind a workshop facilitator you imagine yourself to be, as far as students are concerned you have control and so they are vulnerable. Many students are unhappy with workshops as a teaching method whatever you do. By asking people to engage with a style of teaching they may never have met before, you are threatening; in particular, you threaten students with exposure as frauds. For most students are sure that they do not study properly, and do not wish to take part in any situation which shows this up. It is worth spending time considering why students might find participation difficult, and this means getting out among your classes and listening to what they are saying. Developing an understanding makes it easier to teach: dyslexic students, for example, can be stricken with paralysing terror if presented with an exercise that includes a timed period allotted to reading. It is worth being realistic about how there are always a few students present who will hate being made to learn in these ways – as one complained to me very recently, 'these workshops are hopeless, all you ever do is draw stuff out of me and make me work with other people'. Anyone who has suffered humiliation for prolonged periods of their life, either at home or at school (or sometimes both), will find this kind of co-operative learning particularly testing.

Exercise 9.1 is a reminder of how uncomfortable workshops can be and is called 'Turn-offs'. 'Joining in' is considered an essential prerequisite to active and effective learning, so enthusiasm can blind workshop leaders to how much they humiliate participants. This exercise can be done by tutors, counsellors and students, but is most easily done if groups include a range of experiences:

Exercise 9.1: Turn-offs

1. In small groups, think back over as many courses as you can remember being on where 'ice-breaking' exercises were used. If you have never experienced one, try to think of any of which you have heard, or work out the details of ice-breakers described by others in your group.
2. What did you dislike about those exercises, or what would you dislike if made to do them?
3. Which exercises would you describe as 'turn-offs' and what was it about them that turns you off?

Common elements that cause 'ice-breakers' to become 'turn-offs' are to do with humiliation, uninvited physical contact, exposure, expectations of trust before bonds have been built up, and rapid regression to childhood feelings of loss of control. When working with participants who are highly experienced in workshop methods, Exercise 9.1 can uncover distress in apparently assertive individuals who have not previously felt able to analyse or express these feelings.

Workshops fit uncomfortably into a competitive system as they demand that people suddenly start to share their hard-earned knowledge. With increased numbers of students reading for degrees it has become more pressing that teaching staff adopt different methods within their institutions, and students may become more accustomed to workshop-type methods.

However, few students arrive at university with the experience of sharing with strangers how they go about study or understanding that they can learn a great deal from fellow students. One of the first steps towards independent learning is to understand that 'study' cannot be taught in a lecture-style course, rather practice and time play a large part in implementing what you know in your head about ways of studying.

Organizing open access courses

Staff often do not wish to run workshops on study because they, too, are ambivalent about examining the 'nuts and bolts' of their trade. Some see it as unworthy of attention while others fear that teaching students about study is a form of cheating, and, as with counselling, will give some students an unfair advantage over others. Many fear their own ignorance, and are unsure how to integrate study work with course content. It becomes easier to call in an outsider, for whom the problem is one of how worthwhile or satisfying it is to separate how people study from the content of courses. For the workshop organizer, being called in as the 'expert' by an academic department means reinforcing the notion of study as something separate to course content, and an issue with which real academics do not engage.

Open access courses, away from departments, offer students the opportunity to drop in and out as it suits them, a level of anonymity. They are outside those situations in which they are usually assessed, which can offset many of the participants' worst fears about study workshops. There may be some specific groups across an institution who share identifiable needs, and the arrangement and content of courses is improved if they are designed in consultation with members of the groups concerned. It is never easy to arrange follow-up work with open access courses, as the clientele fluctuates, hence these courses are best used to provide introductory study work.

Workshop goals in open access courses may well be more general than those attached to specific courses: so, for example, one may wish to alert students to issues involved in reading, or to make more explicit some common experiences in writing. Advertising is both time-consuming and expensive, but of itself works to normalize the idea that students should commonly think about how they study, rather than wait until a problem has emerged. Arranging a course with a series of different facilitators allows students access to a range of approaches, which combats the view of study as a set of hard and fast rules.

Which sessions you decide to run will reflect your own views on what is relevant, as well as reflecting your budget and who is available to take sessions. At each session there will be students who are struggling with their work generally and are likely to need more time and assistance than can be offered in a public workshop, and part of a course organizer's role is to be available to them. Workshops, of necessity, simplify issues and can leave people feeling highly anxious if they lack confidence and feel surrounded by glib answers and clever students. Allowing time for individual conversations at the end of a session is essential, whether or not you were the facilitator.

Running study courses away from departments allows students a level of anonymity, which encourages openness. But for the facilitator this means teaching complete strangers without the prospect of building up relationships. So facilitators will appear didactic, whatever their intentions: even in the most open sessions people will assume that you are teaching a system of study.

Basic attitudes

Most forms of teaching are content-based, but workshops focus on *process*. To run workshops effectively you must want to provide a situation which enables people to learn. This student-centred approach is based on certain principles: that people learn effectively by joining in actively, by building on their own experience, and by sharing their knowledge with other people.

To run workshops you need to believe that people's experiences are worthwhile and of value. Also, you need to think that it is important for students (of whatever age and educational experience) to develop their own styles of working, understanding and developing strategies for overcoming academic challenges. It helps if you get real pleasure out of seeing other people develop, rather than viewing them as blank sheets on which you can imprint your 'correct' understanding.

Workshops might be challenging, but they also need to be safe for the participant. Ideally, no one should be put on the spot, embarrassed, made to feel foolish or to go further in speech or actions than they feel comfortable with. This requires sensitivity and imagination in producing simple exercises which allow people to join in. As well as the anxieties already mentioned as present for students when attending study workshops, Gibbs (1981: 89) has argued that a sense of safety is an essential ingredient in enabling adults to accept change: that those students with most doubts about the efficacy of their approach to study are often most entrenched, and most in need of encouragement to flexibility and change.

There are many games and exercises which can be borrowed and adapted. They tend to become elaborate, and it is easy to lose sight of your most valuable resource – the participants. Some of the most successful workshops can be run with pencils, scrap paper, and active, enthusiastic participants. One of the biggest tests of a workshop leader's confidence is to let go of an elaborately planned agenda, and allow a constructive discussion to take over. This is not easy to do if course content dictates progress. Whatever activities are decided upon, one golden rule is: if you are slightly uncomfortable taking part in an exercise, then the participants are sure to be uncomfortable.

A simple sort of exercise is one in which participants can draw upon their own knowledge to discuss with others, without having to make personal confessions about their own experiences. Exercise 9.2 is of this type and can be used by staff, students, tutors and counsellors.

Exercise 9.2: Skills required

Ask people to sit in groups. Give each group blank cards or paper, and ask them (the exercise leader should have worked through this exercise already) to write down (quickly) individual skills they feel undergraduates need in order to complete a degree well (15 minutes).

Then collate the group's agreed skills, and discuss them with three thoughts in mind: what did they miss out, what did I miss out and what overlaps? (15 minutes). Some skills which a list might be expected to include are:

- working independently;
- self-discipline;
- self-motivation;
- effective organization of work;
- library skills;
- the ability to discuss in groups;
- researching complex material;
- writing clearly;
- working to deadlines;
- working quickly;
- experience of group work;
- summarizing material;
- thinking clearly and critically;
- offering coherent arguments.

Group skills (on the more complete, collated list) according to what is essential, what is desirable and what is not really necessary, and explain why you have assigned a skill to that group (30 minutes).

This exercise allows people to reflect on skills needed, without publicly questioning what it is they are aiming towards. As 'homework' one can suggest to students that they spend time privately thinking about which skills are relevant to their studies and ambitions.

Giving instructions for group work

Good presentations and workshops can be undermined when unclear instructions are given for small (or leaderless) group work. This arises out of: nervousness about tying down group discussion too firmly in advance; and concern about facilitators appearing too directive. What can emerge are indecisive, unclear instructions given in a manner which suggests that the subsequent work is not of much importance. If you believe that group work is a valuable way of learning, then it does not make sense to give the opposite message to participants, who rightly expect workshop leaders to plan constructive activities.

The time to overcome these problems is in the early stages of planning. The workshop's agreed aims will provide a blueprint which can be translated into a short list of issues participants will address. Each activity should have an essential part to play in developing these issues or themes – so the presenters will have a clear picture in their minds as to what they are asking participants to do, and why it is being done in a particular way. Group work, then, should have an active part in carrying a workshop forward rather than just being something which is always done at a certain stage in the proceedings. Your aims for group exercises need to be turned into a clear, concise set of instructions made up of few words which are short and easy for you to say. Back them up with an overhead projector slide or flipchart on which are written the same words that you have planned to say.

While the instructions should be short and clear, they also need to be open-ended so that discussion is not closed down in advance of group work. Some participants panic when instructions are given, out of nervousness, which can encourage facilitators to expand on their original words. These extra words usually add to the general chaos – it is more helpful to repeat your original words and point to the OHP slide or flipchart. As the group(s) begin to settle, then go round and check that participants know what they are doing.

Tutoring small groups

When workshops either form a leaderless group or break into smaller groups, the facilitator has usually set an exercise or task. The role of tutor is not an essential part of this, but there are times when such a role can be helpful:

1. Not everyone is used to a workshop mode of learning. Rather than being irritated with such inexperience it can help to join a group, temporarily, when it is clear that participants are struggling to understand what is expected of them. The role then is one of asking open-ended questions which help people to get under way, and it is possible to withdraw quietly as participants begin to address each other rather than the tutor.
2. Occasional intervention is required where it is obvious that a group cannot control a powerful member who is 'hijacking' a session. If the session is part of training for committee work, management or counselling, then a group would be expected to sort this out themselves. However, with a mixed group of students concerned, for example, with learning about writing, intervention might be required to enable the majority to gain fully from the session.
3. It is likely that you may be running a workshop because of your expertise in a specific area, and people will be attending because of this. Spending time with each group gives participants the chance to ask questions they would not put when sitting in the full group.

4. In mixed groups the experience and problems participants bring will vary, and joining groups gives you the chance to respond to these specific needs.

There is a delicate balance to be struck with group work between appearing like a hovering bird of prey, about to swoop on a nervous quarry, and the alternative extreme which is to withdraw altogether, even physically leaving the room. It requires judgement on your part as to which end of the continuum you are moving towards and it might be that your decision to participate with groups is based on a dominant mood in a group, with individuals feeling differently about your presence or absence. In all the cases described as requiring your presence, the style of tutoring should be a quiet one (although firm in the case of 2), temporarily joining in as another member of the group but including questions which enable the most reticent to join in. Questions should be open and put in a manner which invites response, which means actually being interested in the answers rather than planning your next words.

Exercise 9.3 depends on the success of small-group work and gives an exercise leader the opportunity to join in with small groups and encourage discussion.

Exercise 9.3: Running into trouble

In small groups come up with a list of three reasons why a student might run into trouble with university work (15 minutes).

Collate the reasons agreed by different groups: how similar, how different are they? Are the reasons course/study-related or 'personal'?

Discuss the results in plenary session: Are people saying that emotional matters have an impact on academic/intellectual performance? Are they separate areas of life? What are the processes at work which make one impact on the other?

In this exercise a facilitator can assess how useful a plenary session will be by joining small groups, and may decide to return the final discussion to small groups. To avoid confusion when instructing people to return to discussion in groups, this is one occasion where a 'back-up' OHP slide with the final questions printed on can be useful, allowing the workshop leader to be responsive to circumstances by preparing an alternative strategy.

Presentations

Presentations are often used at the beginning of a workshop, or as an introduction to a new section of a workshop. A presentation can be a talk, a video, a role-play or a team role-play. It is used to focus on the issues surrounding a topic or a particular setting – management, committees or interviews are some common settings highlighted by this method. Problems presented are usually complex ones about which one hopes members of the workshop will vary in their opinions.

Another element in presentations is skill development. So, for example, where it is your intention that participants will learn clear messages about good and bad ways of going about an interview, then a subsequent exercise will analyse the presentation. When introducing the presentation, you may ask participants to identify with the role-play counsellor.

Presentations can become highly complex, and need to be rigorously thought out in advance: the timing, the equipment needed and the aims of the exercise. It is wise to check out the room to be used in advance: if there is an audience of 70 and an L-shaped room, then you have a problem. Some presentations are 'cumulative', stopping at intervals for participant exercises, building audience responses into the next section of the presentation. To avoid the whole exercise falling apart it is useful to have one member of the team assigned to giving exercise instructions clearly to the audience.

There is much confusion about 'role-plays', which are often used as a form of play-acting. Anyone involved in role-plays needs time to debrief if necessary, and this is hard to do if an audience is waiting expectantly for the next part of the workshop (it also looks odd to those in the audience who are unaware of the need to debrief). The use of role-plays needs careful thinking if you work in a team and are to avoid abusing the good will of co-presenters. According to Rogers (1989: 136–7), asking students to join in role-plays as part of an academic course is often feared as tutors are nervous that too much emotion will pour out; however, her experience is that the opposite is more likely, that students may not want to step out of 'the conventionally passive student role' for what may seem like amateur dramatics. As she says, if it is difficult to persuade students to do and requires special pleading on the tutor's part, then role-play is probably not an appropriate method for your course.

Playing to the gallery

Running a workshop is a stressful form of teaching as it does not allow the levels of control most teachers are used to; nor does it allow a facilitator the authority derived from being the 'master' of the workshop's content. By definition, a workshop is based on the experience and knowledge of the participants while the facilitator is the person who provides the stepping-stones which might enable people to move to greater understanding and awareness. There are workshop participants who do not like this form of teaching, and will take out their frustration and anger on the workshop leader. Similarly, the facilitator has no sense of safety and can develop strategies for 'hiding' behind complex exercises which feel safe.

There is a temptation to design workshops which you know 'work': that is, where, rather like giving coloured crayons to children, experience shows that you will get least flak. If, in addition, you are working freelance and wish to be invited back, then the temptation is even greater. This tendency is reinforced with on-the-spot appraisal forms, which can act as a 'clapometer'. Popularity cannot be the same as efficacy, and with study it can be weeks and months later before individuals absorb and benefit from new ideas. I am all in favour of people enjoying workshops and earning a living, but it is easy to become trapped into running workshops which do not interest you and to collude with audiences in avoiding the difficult issues.

If you usually do 'one-off' workshops, which allow little opportunity to build up a relationship with a group or to find out what individual needs might be, there is every good reason to design workshops which distance you further and further from audiences. When visiting a department or institution, the facilitator can provide a focus as an outsider against which the group identifies itself, and makes you the target of all the discontent which cannot be expressed within the work setting. While it is a part of the facilitator's role to 'draw fire', it is also wearing and exhausting if experienced without colleagues to back you up and without occasional positive feedback for yourself. Keeping participants busy with a whirling round of role-plays, complex exercises, community singing and dancing bears is not always a good enough substitute for honestly addressing the issues, even though it is a tempting solution.

Breaking out of that pattern is frightening and is best done with workshops on which your future income does not hang; and preferably if you present the workshop with at least one other person. One of the facilitator's roles is to talk to participants at the end of a workshop, and frequently the most articulate of the discontented will leave you with the impression that the session was a disaster. It is only later that facilitators find that other people have benefited from a session. Sharing the burden with a compatible colleague removes a lot of tension; if this is not an option, then a friend or colleague who understands workshops and is willing to talk things over with you (especially afterwards) in a supportive way is an invaluable ally.

Rounding-off group work and exercises

A workshop should be about people learning from themselves and each other by actively taking part in discussion and exercises; workshop leaders abandon a didactic expert role in favour of providing a situation which enables themselves and others to learn. Participants have the right to expect a 'safe' environment, which includes expecting facilitators to understand what they are asking of a group and why they are asking it. Having a constructive sense of purpose is not the same as deciding, in advance, what conclusions you intend participants to draw, what solutions they should all agree on or precisely the route by which they achieve personal answers.

Leaving small-group work 'hanging', without any attempt to round off at the end of a period can make some participants feel that the exercise is not integrated into the whole session. This non-use of group work is a leftover from the early days of workshops when, in enthusiasm for people learning actively, it was seen as an intrusion if the facilitator spoke. Depending on the overall size of the group, using a flipchart to record what groups have covered is one solution. It provides facilitators with a temptation to slide into a pedagogic mode, but the actual role is one of filleter, allowing the reporters to describe their group's work in full while picking out the core issues. A flipchart is not essential, but the pattern remains useful as long as the facilitator allows sufficient time for each group to describe the *process* by which they reached their conclusions and allows for infinite variety between groups.

'Reporting back' is a useful time for skills development where people are learning about speaking in public or management training. Where these skills are not essential and the overall group size is too big, team facilitators need to be briefed to go round groups to get a feel for what has been happening, and can do the reporting back if this seems helpful. Where small-group work is to remain private, a tutor or tutors can go round quietly at the end of sessions to explain that the time is over, and to ask general questions (such as whether the session was helpful, whether there were any surprises, and so on).

Good manners, ethics and assumptions

Workshop leaders and organizers are responsible for ensuring that while participants are challenged and stretched, trainers do not bully, hector, harass, embarrass, humiliate, show up, put on the spot, force disclosure from, or physically touch, threaten or intimidate participants. All abusers of adults or children justify such behaviour as being for the good of the victim or their own fault, and any trainers who so rationalize abusive behaviour should be regarded with suspicion. Adults have often experienced violence and humiliation in their early schooling, and misuse of power in teaching does not facilitate their learning – it merely causes pleasure to bullies.

Any exercise which obliges people to examine private experience in public is potentially abusive, so the usual method is to ask people to look outside themselves by thinking of others. Exercise 9.4 is underpinned by a shared experience for people of all ages, and that is being a new student. It is potentially painful and unpleasant to examine publicly what this felt like, yet it might be appropriate to heighten staff awareness of the process or to encourage students to review the experience.

Exercise 9.4: Giving advice

In small groups, agree a list of six pieces of essential advice for a new student, to enable them to successfully complete their first year (20 minutes). It is for the group to agree between them what 'success' means.

When, eventually, a list is agreed, ask groups to swap their lists, then interpret what assumptions about university life underlie the pieces of advice they have been given (20–30 minutes, depending on how groups are proceeding).

Compare the different groups' analyses of the views of university life and discuss in plenary session (anything up to 30 minutes, depending on how it proceeds).

The assumptions are not necessarily wrong, but they may be unquestioned.

Workshop leaders are facilitators, which means that they enable adults to learn. To do this, they need to be interested in and aware of the barriers to adults' learning, in order to design exercises which provide stepping-stones to learning and to ensure an appropriate environment for learning. An 'appropriate environment' grows out of a central tenet of person-centred learning, which is respect for fellow adults. So, while people may be testing their own boundaries and experimenting with new ideas, they should do so in a safe and unthreatening setting. An exercise which is safe among strangers may be a disaster with colleagues, and the workshop leader should know the difference.

Experiential training is particularly relevant where the subject matter is potentially more emotional than usual (all workshops should engage participants' feelings as well as thinking): on counselling courses, social work training, responding to sexual abuse and so on. The valuation of the worth of students' experience and knowledge requires their total participation, emotionally as well as intellectually. It requires the same on the part of facilitators, who need to have allowed room in their lives away from workshops to explore their own attitudes and experiences, emotional and academic. Woolfe (1992: 7) has well described the role of a facilitative trainer:

> The term (often used as a synonym for the idea of 'enabling') implies a commitment to a client- or student-centred form of relationship or to operating from within the other person's frame of reference. This is not the same as non-involvement or non-participating, or withdrawing from responsibility for establishing a structure, framework and boundaries within which a group of people can work.

Insight into one's own emotional history allows one to be facilitative in the presence of other people's personal struggles and helps one provide the supports necessary for learning and change. 'Stepping-stones' are again needed to ensure that the majority of people can have access to learning via a workshop session, and are not excluded by their own emotional history which may make participation difficult.

Another means of using highly personal thoughts as the basis for an exercise is to maintain privacy by ensuring that the thoughts always remain anonymous. So, Exercise 9.5, about daydreams and frustration, can be used with staff or students, and can be used among people who know each other. Instructions written on an overhead projector or on prepared slips of paper are useful ways of reinforcing the anonymous nature of the exercise.

Exercise 9.5: Daydreams

Write on a piece of paper any daydream you can remember having or can imagine yourself as likely to have had when starting a new course (any course at any level); and make sure that your daydream is not identifiable.

The daydreams are then collected up, and the class is divided into groups of a reasonable size for discussion.

Each group is (verbally) given a daydream: they must respond to the student who, one imagines, has come to see you because they now feel they should change or give up their course. Given the secret daydream: how do you think the student might respond to this situation?

Groups are given the rest of the daydreams, one by one, until the pile is finished.

Complete the exercise with a group discussion of the *process* the groups went through in deciding on their responses – but start by collating the daydreams, they usually have a lot in common.

Other aspects of power and its abuse in workshops focus on how 'voluntary' the participants' presence actually is. For example, in a recession, most personnel development courses allow for limited choices about attendance. If people's employment and promotion are on the line, then there are severe limits to the amount of personal disclosure or insecurity included in a session. Likewise, if you mark students' work, then you should think very carefully about what you ask them to discuss openly in workshop sessions. What seems commonplace to you can be experienced by participants as highly personal or uncomfortable in the presence of a powerful figure.

Learning should be challenging, and can affect adults profoundly. Yet participants need to retain a sense of control, even if they are being stretched and trying new activities or ideas. Workshop leaders should be aware that while participants' defensiveness may hamper progress, most adults have defences for very good reasons. Trust must always be earned, and the belief that you are a good trainer with the participants' best interests at heart is not enough reason to demand that they abandon personal autonomy. One 'ice-breaking' exercise from the 1960s and 1970s involved participants crawling on their hands and knees across a room. To achieve this, they had physically to interweave with others doing the same along the length of the room. This was based on naive assumptions about why people are not physically open and assumed a certain physical fitness, allowing for neither age nor disability.

Undergraduates are as likely as the rest of the population to have suffered rape, incest, physical assault and extreme humiliation during their lives. While few would use such an exercise now, the same assumptions are made more covertly. Workshops should enable adults to learn, whatever their backgrounds and experiences, and to participate regardless of physical or mobility problems.

Workshops for students tend to be run on the mistaken assumption that students are a homogeneous group. Exercises which ask participants to move around a room, move quickly, climb on chairs, or pick out other people in the room, cannot be done by blind or partially sighted students or by those with any mobility problem. Similarly, exercises which are meant to be amusing can be offensive – for example, making assumptions about sexual experience and orientation or discussion of underwear. This sort of approach causes severe embarrassment to many Western students, but ensures that Muslim students have to leave the room and that they never again attend a study workshop.

Residential courses can allow a group to bond, people to join in exercises which they might not otherwise do if on 'home territory', and fosters concentration, so allowing rapid personal development. However, residential courses also induce a feeling of being 'trapped' and so replicate feelings of helplessness experienced elsewhere in life. Asking participants to reveal themselves to fellow students, colleagues, friends or employers can be destructive of everyday work and social relationships.

Respect for each other as fellow learners requires movement away from the assumption that being in the role of teacher implies superiority of age, wisdom, values or taste. Mastery of one's subject does not lead to mastery of fellow humans who wish to learn about your subject. Most students at university wish to engage with what Kolb called 'social knowledge', wanting more than the accreditation of what they have done already; they want access to a body of knowledge and theory hitherto unavailable to them. To do so is a highly personal process played out publicly in pressured and bureaucratic institutions. In the final chapter I ask if there are other strategies for offering study support, beyond the open access workshops touched on in this chapter and the response to individual crises considered in the rest of this book.

10

Structures

This book has presented a particular approach to helping undergraduates who face study problems. It is one which puts students' needs first, rather than teaching a predecided set of study techniques. This style is grounded in three combined beliefs: that people bring their prior experiences to learning at university; that learning is an emotional as well as an intellectual matter; and that the social environment of the institutions in which adults study exercises a strong influence over the process of learning. Usually the aim of my early meetings with students is to untangle crises: either because they are no longer working or because they are not meeting university standards. Whatever it is that needs to be done by students, the early stages of study counselling are focused on fairly crude strategies for changing the immediate situation. Those strategies provide a grounding for future developments because they are set within the context of the student's life, interests and definitions of the situation.

Personal contacts and relationships make an astonishing difference to how study crises are met and challenges overcome, and awareness of their importance has been with us for a long time. Whenever there is significant change in the system of higher education, there then follows a wave of research into university teaching and student learning. Nisbet and Welsh (1976) wrote of the importance of individual contacts during the last wave of research, following the expansion of universities in the 1960s. In attempting to predict which students were likely to fail they recruited to their research project students in trouble with their studies, only to find that their work then improved. The authors came to the conclusion that it had been the interest expressed in students' progress which altered their academic performance. Unsurprising, then, that 'study' is an important part of what student counsellors have traditionally offered to students, and it is working with academic problems which makes counselling in universities a different activity to counselling anywhere else. Along with student counsellors, there is a reservoir of experience of 'study counselling' or tutoring among teaching staff, personal tutors, chaplains, library staff, research assistants, postgraduates, debt counsellors, student union staff and many, many more. In a university it is right that 'study' is the property of all, yet with time increasingly limited there is the danger that students will lose the range of informal supports previously available to them. In so doing, help becomes available only when students have been diagnosed as needy and hence 'problematized', with referral on to an 'expert' as the next stage. The professionalization of care may be necessary up to a point, but it always carries the inherent danger that 'normal' academic progress is assumed so that we can define deviancy. This is both an unrealistic and an unhelpful distortion of how human beings go about the complex business of learning.

A major misapprehension about academic work is that reading and writing happen once and straight off, and if not then this is a sign of something seriously wrong. The fantasy is that the good student sits down to read, understands a text in one go and remembers essential detail after taking notes. Likewise, the idea that it is possible to translate what is in one's head into clear writing, also in one go, sets up ridiculous expectations. The translation of a hazy mental picture into a piece of academic writing which communicates clearly is an arduous process, whatever the subject matter. This expectation of 'one sitting' is partly due to the speed at which students rocket through degrees: three years maximum for the bulk of degrees is commonplace. This reflects the notion that all adult learners need is to pour in more information, and that the only education issues at this level are pedagogical ones concerning how slickly the message is packaged and then passed from teacher to taught. In such a climate any hiccup is experienced as a problem rather than as an academic challenge, and any problem is cranked up into a major crisis. Add to this the recent changes in universities, with increasing numbers of students fighting for limited resources, including staff time, and the result is frustration and disappointment with the undergraduate experience. Little time is available in such an environment to build the confidence needed to confront academic challenges.

My emphasis is on helping students marshal their own resources in the face of challenges, learning to study with confidence by getting to know themselves better as learners. This means students grappling with the content of their courses, trying to come to a personal understanding of topics without being browbeaten by lack of confidence or alien vocabulary. It is some years now since Svensson (1984) differentiated between study techniques (such as note-taking and underlining) and skills, and wrote: 'To see these techniques as skills in themselves is misleading, for this has the effect of isolating them from the student's thinking about the content of the study task of which they form a part' (1984: 68). To talk, then, only of 'study techniques' is to offer a limited vision of what can be derived from academic work; techniques of study are used in order to further understanding, not as ends to be achieved in themselves. 'Study skills', in Svensson's sense, are a part of academic endeavour, not an optional extra, for the two are inseparable: course content and its means of expression and understanding are both aspects of learning. In a system which is highly competitive and pressured, with most students expecting to graduate within three years of starting a degree, it makes sense that we offer help and support when study goes wrong. Individuals will always need help, but there are wider structural questions about whether there are additional ways of encouraging students to develop academically as well as responding to crises as they arise or teaching 'techniques' in isolation from course content.

It is a truism to say that academic work is central to university life, and therefore 'study' belongs to all who teach, research or offer support in universities. Allowing for one strategy only in response to students' wide-ranging study needs is ingenuous in complex institutions. To run an effective study support programme in a university requires close liaison between three areas: up-to-date research into teaching and learning; staff development work to foster changes in methods of teaching and in providing an appropriate environment; and help given to students who have run into trouble. This book has, for the most part, concentrated on helping students whose degree-level studies have gone awry, and who may have stopped working altogether. However, the thinking underlying this approach has implications for general teaching and fits within that tradition usually known as 'student-centred learning'. It begs the question whether these problems would have developed so severely had the teaching been different.

Teaching

As student numbers increase, people have become aware of the need for teaching repertoires which include more than just seminars and lectures; departments need to have a range of experience to call upon among their members. With outside pressure making staff appraisal more usual and with increases in student class sizes, reflection on teaching aims and practice has become more commonplace. The responses to these new challenges do not necessarily lie solely with the abilities of individual teachers, but with overall departmental aims and strategies. There are two sets of teaching options for departments: one is to make some changes in teaching methods to encourage student participation; and the other is to develop an entirely different approach to course design, with content, teaching styles and study-skill development integrated.

Of the former, many staff have developed, privately, a variety of ways of handling seminars which could be described as 'workshop methods', but they probably do not recognize them as such. Habeshaw *et al.* have produced a series of clear publications offering a wide selection of suggestions which individual lecturers across a range of subjects could introduce into their teaching, some fairly revolutionary and others only mildly so (see, for example, Habeshaw *et al.* 1984; 1987; Gibbs and Habeshaw 1988). The exercises they suggest encompass the view that students are autonomous learners, hence they do not assume one correct mode of study or academic activity. My own belief is that lecturers need to have confidence in what they do best already in teaching, and that this provides a happier basis for experimenting with new methods, rather than being faced with yet another set of pressures to become something which seems alien. It is not helpful, for example, to push project-based work simply because it processes the maximum number of students with minimum staff contact. Rather, project work calls for particular skills on the part of tutors in providing students with the stepping-stones by which they come to understand group work, private research and co-operative writing. To offer project work to students requires an honest assessment of the teaching styles available in a given department, for tutors need to be particularly adept at offering mediation when group dynamics goes wrong. To make academic work conducive and effective for both teacher and taught, what needs to be acknowledged is that teaching methods are not 'givens' but are evolving and changing, responsive to conditions and circumstances.

So Gibbs (1992) has argued that it is not worth holding on to the traditional seminar, that while the problems of group dynamics can be overcome by a range of devices (putting people into pairs to debate, for example) this does not address the belief that seminars somehow develop participants' presentational abilities. If the aim is to ensure that students have an hour in smallish groups to explore a topic, then the strategies referred to by Gibbs become useful replacements for sitting around waiting for one or two people to break embarrassed silences. If presentation is what it is about, then full facilities should be available for this along with tutoring which encourages students in the skills required. Presentation tends, at the moment, to be a specialist activity in marketing departments or on design courses, where specific work situations are envisaged and rehearsed, and the presentation itself is assessed, not its content alone. As Gibbs (1992: 5) says, to do this generally, 'we would provide training in presentation skills and not just expect students to be able to do it by osmosis as a result of sitting in so many brilliant lectures'. Whatever the intentions, however, Gibbs (1992: 4) also points out that universities have been built with the assumption that teaching 'happened largely in small groups in lecturers' offices'. Tutors who are not housed in a lecturer's study constantly fight against room-booking systems, missing equipment and architecture when running seminars and small-group work, and staff who are trying to change their methods of teaching will come up against similar barriers.

An alternative approach to course design, in contrast, would start with a list of the specific topics to be included in a course, followed by designing how it will be taught; hence, one's status as departmental subject specialist can remain unsullied, whatever co-operative input there might be to overall teaching strategies. The design of teaching integrates study-skill development (in Svensson's sense of the phrase) with core topics, working to implement a list of skills which has already been agreed by the department. Around these topics students would be expected to explore by locating and using different sorts of information, or applying knowledge in given situations. But before deciding how to teach course content and study matters, departments need to agree what general skills and achievements students should be encouraged to work towards. The process of discussion and argument can be revolutionary for departments, as some will find agreement hard to reach. The usual list would go something like this:

Personal	*Skills*
organizing time	writing reports
organizing resources	writing essays
management of jobs	oral presentation
management of projects	giving and taking instructions accurately
group co-operation	reading – general
organizing material	finding information
flexibility	abstracting information
purposive working	interpreting data
awareness of learning	note-taking
processes	literacy
self-appraisal	numeracy
autonomy	computer literacy
self-starting	use of necessary materials – e.g., tables,
initiative	graphs
judgement/decisiveness	self-discipline/clear expression

These lists tend to reflect wishful thinking, and provide a time for grumbles about how all students spell so badly these days. The final list must be one which can be translated into action, for it should form the groundplan around which teaching is designed. So, if there is no one on the team who can find a way of teaching which might develop the skill or quality concerned then it must be dropped as an intention, and the course cannot be evaluated as falling short on that specific intention if there was no means, in practice, of attempting to achieve it.

Encouraging independence in study is, in part, about structural decisions made by departments and universities, and cannot be left to individual teaching styles alone. A lot of material is now available to help lecturers and departments develop teaching methods which encourage independence in student learning. So, for example, Magin *et al.* (1993) have written a comprehensive, readable pamphlet called *Strategies for Increasing Students' Independence* which is easy to dip into and organized in such a way that one can quickly find what one needs, from reducing student dependence on lectures through to laboratory work and computer packages. In its user-friendliness, it reflects awareness that not all staff are interested in or have time to wade through educational theory in order to innovate in their own teaching to meet changes in the system. A prototype of this approach is similarly accessible on the subject of improving student writing (Nightingale 1986), in which the author simply and directly explains to non-specialist staff the means and advantages of addressing student writing as an integral part of academic teaching. So she makes simple statements which imply straightforward action for practitioners, yet her work is drawn from an understanding of the complexities of student learning and student needs. So: 'Part of clarifying expectations is identifying models of good expression in the literature of our areas and calling these to students' attention' (1986: 28).

For educationists this style of writing provides the challenge of presenting their research to non-specialists without over-simplifying the content to the point where the central message becomes bland or meaningless. In writing for non-specialists, educationists always run the risk of losing credibility in their 'home' disciplines, whose members expect a particular style of language use; however, it remains a central task to translate their own research into a form which is comprehensible to practitioners. The availability of existing research means that lecturers do not have to reinvent the wheel in isolation, but can learn from what others have already done. Most institutions now employ someone with expertise in these matters to coordinate staff development initiatives, who should be available to offer advice and information to departments, as well as arranging training for individuals.

Whose degree is it anyway?

My role is to help individuals glean the maximum personal intellectual development they can, as they pass at speed through highly structured institutions of mass higher education. Study counselling is one means of helping students to leave university, with or without a degree, with greater confidence in their abilities, increased awaresess of themselves both intellectually and emotionally, and with insight into how they have met and overcome academic challenges. While universities hand out thousands of degrees every year, most students only get one opportunity in a lifetime to study for a degree – it is *their* chance and it matters to them.

While educationists are trying to foster independent learning, students often have a sense of grievance that no one in universities is interested in them or their work. Unlike the popular image of university life, there is no one person who cares about an individual student's ideas or development. This does not mean that all students expect to have their hands held, just that the isolation and loneliness of university study hits new students like a cold wind. Being thrown in unsupported does not, of itself, foster effective approaches to study, and merely ensures that those who know how to negotiate university on arrival flourish while others lose confidence. It is always easier for students to approach agencies for help if they can present a clear, apparently containable problem, but study problems have an impact on other areas of life, and people bring to study all that they are in experience and expectations. Ratigan (1989: 158) well summarizes a typical situation, where due to the pressure to gain places in higher education teachers have, inadvertently, encouraged teacher-dependent approaches to study which are inappropriate for the independent work and personal characteristics demanded for success in higher education. This kind of situation is not alleviated by teaching study-skills techniques alone, although the introduction of new ideas can come via suggested techniques. These new ideas will only be useful within a context of personal growth, in confidence particularly, and increased flexibility in the student's views of academic work and the process of learning. This does not imply that anyone who has gained academic success is well adjusted; rather, it means that, when faced with severe study problems, the undergraduate must look to the whole of their life when developing strategies to overcome these problems.

Studying for a degree gets wedged in between a range of big 'life' decisions: whatever age the student, the decision to register for a degree marks a change in life, a cutting-off point from much of what went before. The choice of subject is a personal statement about individuals, how they view themselves, the world and their futures. People meet and part from partners before, after and during university studies, at whatever stage in their lives they have started as undergraduates. Severe recessions wither job prospects, and cause fear about the future, so that students spend the final year of study struggling with major questions about the rest of their lives. These decisions are exciting, somewhat like a roller-coaster ride, liberating and funny, but when the central justification for being at university (study) feels out of control, then the same 'life' decisions crowd in as unpleasant and frightening. Study techniques which are supposed to be about efficiency hide deeply personal questions. Time management, for example, is not just about matching tasks to time available, but about setting one's priorities to ensure that the things in life you value the most are happening. That means knowing yourself quite well: what drains your energy unconstructively; and what brings you pleasure and recharges batteries. I have noticed how often students who have built up a backlog of work feel obliged to 'timetable out' sport because it feels like play, hence hard to justify if deadlines are not being met. Yet without the opportunity to let off steam, race around outside, join in team events, the same students get increasingly sluggish, depressed and unhappy, and the likelihood of completing work becomes more remote. Before drawing up efficient and worthy timetables, people need to examine what role activities play in their lives, or they might lose something of importance.

When starting at university students try hard to fit into an existing structure, leaving behind numerous activities which have been central to their pre-university lives. These can be anything: sewing, knitting, designing, painting, horse-riding, cycling, music-making, composing, singing, walking, shopping, cooking, drawing, voluntary work, listening to the radio, reading for pleasure, going to the cinema, walking the dog, talking to family, listening to the children . . . . The list is endless, and many activities are too expensive for student budgets, but within a short space of time people feel wound up, frustrated and uncomfortable. Knowing that one should be grateful for the expensive and privileged opportunity of university study does not lessen the sense of living an impoverished life. As students, people may not be able to carry on with exactly the same activities as before, but they do need to replace these with others which bring similar qualities to their lives. Perhaps drawing gave the chance for quiet reflection, concentrating on a non-verbal focus, and students find that without this outlet (or something comparable) they no longer concentrate so well when reading.

Time management is, in reality, finding out what is stopping us from doing what we should do or think we would like to do. A common 'time management' problem is that students cannot say 'no' when a friend knocks on the door to suggest a coffee break. This could mean that the work is boring and people are happy to stop any time; it could mean that a student feels so unlovable that they feel they will never be asked again if they refuse; or it could mean that the student concerned prefers to spend time with people rather than books. The first situation may indicate the wrong choice of courses, tiredness or just the dreary slog that is necessary at some point in most courses of study. The second situation is much wider-ranging, including the whole of how a person perceives themself to be, the little interest they hold for others and the limited power they feel they have. The last situation arises where people know what their priorities are, but these are at odds with other goals (in this case, to get a degree), and a compromise has to be made to allow both to happen at some point in the week. All of them imply questions about how life could be lived:

If you could change any one thing to improve life, what would it be?
If it were a free world, what would you like life to be like?
If you made a list of the things you love to do, what would be on it?
Forgetting everyone else for a moment, what would you like to get out of being a student?

Whenever a backlog of work has built up, people cut out the activities they enjoy most in some kind of punitive revenge on themselves. Very rapidly university becomes a treadmill in which the only reward for completing a piece of work is to start another, and study becomes associated with anxiety and discomfort. Such people might know exactly what they enjoy most in life, what helps them relax and what they would like to get out of university. The question is, rather, why work has to be so painful.

Students do have to fit in with the institution, but have more power to lead lives that suit them individually than is necessarily clear on arrival. Personal development and academic achievement occur in settings which have their own codes, etiquette and social values, which students must unravel if they are not already privy to them. Ratigan (1989: 162) reminds us that counsellors in higher education are privileged because they are regularly presented with 'information not only about their life experiences but also with the impact of institutional processes and other developments on the members of the institution'. These processes and demands are mediated through individual lecturers, who are perceived to be powerful representatives of the institution, and as such they have the capacity to 'invite in' new members, and to exclude others. As we have seen with Nisbet and Welsh's work, personal contact can have an important impact on how students negotiate challenging periods in their studies.

The quality of relationships between all university employees and all students, then, contributes to how successful efforts to develop independence and achievement in student learning are going to be. At the end of the degree, the memories people take away are highly personal: whatever class or subject of degree, students should emerge knowing that the challenges they have overcome are achievements to look back on. Study counselling is part of that educational process which encourages students to graduate with more confidence in their intellectual abilities and awareness of their capabilities than when they arrived.

References

Andresen, L., Nightingale, P., Boud, D. and Magin, D. (1993) *Strategies for Assessing Students*. Birmingham, SEDA Publications.

Becher, T. (1981) Towards a definition of disciplinary cultures, *Studies in Higher Education*, 6(2): 109–22.

Carey, G.V. (1971) *Mind the Stop: A Brief Guide to Punctuation*. London, Penguin (first published by Cambridge University Press in 1939; revised edn 1958).

Dass, R. and Gorman, P. (1985) *How Can I Help?* London, Random House.

Donaldson, M. (1978) *Children's Minds*. London, Fontana.

Egan, G. (1975) *The Skilled Helper: A Model for Systematic Helping and Interpersonal Relating*. Monterey, CA, Brooks/Cole.

Evans, N. (1992) Experiential learning as learning to effect. In R. Barnett (ed.) *Learning to Effect*. Buckingham, SRHE/Open University Press.

Ford, J.K. and Merriman, P. (1990) *The Gentle Art of Listening: Counselling Skills for Volunteers*. London, Bedford Square Press.

Galbraith, D. (1980) The effect of conflicting goals on writing: a case study, *Visible Language*, XIV(4): 364–75.

Gibbs, G. (1981) *Teaching Students to Learn: A Student-Centred Approach*. Milton Keynes, Open University Press.

Gibbs, G. (1992) The seminar, *The New Academic*, 1(3): 4–5.

Gibbs, G. and Habeshaw, T. (1988) *253 Ideas for Your Teaching*. Bristol, Technical and Educational Services.

Gibbs, G., Habeshaw, S. and Habeshaw, T. (1988) *53 Interesting Ways to Assess Your Students*. Bristol, Technical and Educational Services.

Gowers, E. (1979) *The Complete Plain Words*. London, Penguin (first published by HMSO in 1954).

Grierson, M. (1990) A client's experience of success. In D. Mearns and W. Dryden (eds) *Experiences of Counselling in Action*. London, Sage Publications.

Habeshaw, S., Habeshaw, T. and Gibbs, G. (1984) *53 Interesting Things to Do in Your Seminars and Tutorials*. Bristol, Technical and Educational Services.

Habeshaw, T., Habeshaw, S. and Gibbs, G. (1987) *53 Interesting Ways of Helping Your Students to Study*. Bristol, Technical and Educational Services.

Hewitt, J. (1992) *Teach Yourself Relaxation*. Sevenoaks, Hodder & Stoughton.

Hounsell, D. (1984) Essay planning and essay writing, *Higher Education Research and Development*, 3(1): 13–31.

Hughill, B. (1993) Heading for the slums of academe, *The Observer*, 22 August.
Hurst, A. (1993) *Steps towards Graduation: Access to Higher Education for People with Disabilities.* Aldershot, Avebury.
Jackson, B. and Marsden, D. (1968) *Education and the Working Class.* London, Penguin.
Jacobs, M. (1988) *Psychodynamic Counselling in Action.* London, Sage.
Kolb, D.A. (1993) The process of experiential learning. In M. Thorpe, R. Edwards and A. Hanson (eds) *Culture and Processes of Adult Learning.* London, Routledge.
Leach, E.R. (1968) *La Femme Sauvage.* Stevenson Lecture, Bedford College, London.
Leonard, H. (1989) *Out after Dark.* London, Penguin.
Magin, D., Nightingale, P., Andresen, L. and Boud, D. (1993) *Strategies for Increasing Students' Independence.* SCED Paper 77, Birmingham, SEDA Publications.
Martin, T. (1989) *The Strugglers.* Milton Keynes, Open University Press.
Marton, F., Hounsell, D. and Entwistle, N. (1984) *The Experience of Learning.* Edinburgh, Scottish Academic Press.
McLoughlin, B. (1990) The client becomes a counsellor. In D. Mearns and W. Dryden (eds) *Experiences of Counselling in Action.* London: Sage Publications.
Mearns, D. and Dryden, W. (1990) Learning from counselling experiences. In D. Mearns and W. Dryden (eds) *Experiences of Counselling in Action.* London, Sage Publications.
Mearns, D. and Thorne, B. (1988) *Person-Centred Counselling in Action.* London, Sage Publications.
Medawar, P. (1988) *Memoir of a Thinking Radish.* Oxford, Oxford University Press.
Mills, C. Wright (1959) Appendix 'On intellectual craftsmanship'. In *The Sociological Imagination.* New York, Oxford University Press.
Nightingale, P. (1986) *Improving Student Writing.* Green Guide No. 4, University of New South Wales, HERDSA Publications.
Nisbet, J.D. and Welsh, J. (1976) Prediction of failure at university – or failure of prediction?, *British Journal of Educational Psychology*, 46(3).
Peelo, M.T. (1988) Marginality and the experience of women undergraduates. Unpublished PhD thesis, Lancaster University.
Peelo, M. (1994) Martin and the meaning of long division. *Pastoral Care in Education*, 12(1): 19–22.
Ratigan, B. (1989) Counselling in higher education. In W. Dryden, D. Charles-Edwards and R. Woolfe (eds) *Handbook of Counselling in Britain.* London, Tavistock/Routledge.
Renvoize, J. (1993) *Innocence Destroyed: A Study of Child Sexual Abuse.* London, Routledge.
Roberts, R. (1976) *A Ragged Schooling.* London, Fontana.
Rogers, C. (1967) *On Becoming a Person: A Therapist's View of Psychotherapy.* London, Constable (first published in 1961).
Rogers, C. (1983) *Freedom to Learn for the 80s.* Columbus, OH, Charles E. Merrill Publishing Co.
Rogers, J. (1989) *Adults Learning*, 3rd edn. Milton Keynes, Open University Press.
Rowe, D. (1991) *Wanting Everything: The Art of Happiness.* London, Fontana.
Rowntree, D. (1991) *Learn How to Study: A Guide for Students of All Ages.* London, Sphere Books (first published by Macdonald & Co. in 1970; 3rd edn 1988).
Russell, B. (1967) *Introduction to Mathematical Philosophy.* London, George Allen & Unwin (first published in 1919).
Russell, B. (1976) *On Education.* London, Unwin Paperbacks (first published in 1926).

Säljö, R. (1984) Learning from reading. In F. Marton, D. Hounsell and N. Entwistle (eds) *The Experience of Learning.* Edinburgh, Scottish Academic Press.

Sanderson, M. (1975) *The Universities in the Nineteenth Century.* London, Routledge and Kegan Paul.

Sartre, J.-P. (1964) *Words.* London, Penguin.

Sivanandan, A. (1974) Alien gods. In B. Parekh (ed.) *Colour, Culture and Consciousness.* London, George Allen & Unwin.

Steinberg, S. (1974) *The Academic Melting Pot.* New York, McGraw-Hill.

Sullivan, H.S. (1953) *The Interpersonal Theory of Psychiatry.* New York, W.W. Norton and Co.

Svensson, L. (1984) Skill in learning. In F. Marton, D. Hounsell and N. Entwistle (eds) *The Experience of Learning.* Edinburgh, Scottish Academic Press.

Thomas, K. (1990) *Gender and Subject in Higher Education.* Milton Keynes, SRHE/Open University Press.

Walker, M. (1990) *Women in Therapy and Counselling.* Milton Keynes, Open University Press.

Wheeler, S. and Birtle, J. (1993) *A Handbook for Personal Tutors.* Buckingham, SRHE/Open University Press.

White, A. (1986) Education is ordinary: a biographical account. In J. Finch and M. Rustin (eds) *A Degree of Choice? Higher Education and the Right to Learn.* Harmondsworth, Penguin.

Woolfe, R. (1992) Experiential learning in workshops. In T. Hobbs (ed.) *Experiential Training: Practical Guidelines.* London, Tavistock/Routledge.

Index

The Society for Research into Higher Education

The Society for Research into Higher Education exists to stimulate and co-ordinate research into all aspects of higher education. It aims to improve the quality of higher education through the encouragement of debate and publication on issues of policy, on the organization and management of higher education institutions, and on the curriculum and teaching methods.

The Society's income is derived from subscriptions, sales of its books and journals, conference fees and grants. It receives no subsidies, and is wholly independent. Its individual members include teachers, researchers, managers and students. Its corporate members are institutions of higher education, research institutes, professional, industrial and governmental bodies. Members are not only from the UK, but from elsewhere in Europe, from America, Canada and Australasia, and it regards its international work as amongst its most important activities.

Under the imprint *SRHE & Open University Press*, the Society is a specialist publisher of research, having some 45 titles in print. The Editorial Board of the Society's Imprint seeks authoritative research or study in the above fields. It offers competitive royalties, a highly recognizable format in both hard- and paperback and the world-wide reputation of the Open University Press.

The Society also publishes *Studies in Higher Education* (three times a year), which is mainly concerned with academic issues, *Higher Education Quarterly* (formerly *Universities Quarterly*), mainly concerned with policy issues, *Research into Higher Education Abstracts* (three times a year), and *SRHE News* (four times a year).

The Society holds a major annual conference in December, jointly with an institution of higher education. In 1991, the topic was 'Research and Higher Education in Europe', with the University of Leicester. In 1992, it was 'Learning to Effect' with Nottingham Trent University, and in 1993, 'Governments and the Higher Education Curriculum: Evolving Partnerships' at the University of Sussex in Brighton. Future conferences include in 1994, 'The Student Experience' at the University of York.

The Society's committees, study groups and branches are run by the members. The groups at present include:

Teacher Education Study Group
Continuing Education Group
Staff Development Group
Excellence in Teaching and Learning
Women in Higher Education Group

Benefits to members

Individual

Individual members receive:

- *SRHE News*, the Society's publications list, conference details and other material included in mailings.
- Greatly reduced rates for *Studies in Higher Education* and *Higher Education Quarterly*.
- A 35% discount on all Open University Press & SRHE publications.
- Free copies of the Precedings – commissioned papers on the theme of the Annual Conference.
- Free copies of *Research into Higher Education Abstracts*.
- Reduced rates for conferences.
- Extensive contacts and scope for facilitating initiatives.
- Reduced reciprocal memberships.

Corporate

Corporate members receive:

- All benefits of individual members, plus
- Free copies of *Studies in Higher Education*.
- Unlimited copies of the Society's publications at reduced rates.
- Special rates for its members, e.g. to the Annual Conference.

Membership details: SRHE, 344–354 Gray's Inn Road, London, WC1X 8BP, UK. Tel: 071 837 7880
Catalogue: SRHE & Open University Press, Celtic Court, 22 Ballmoor, Buckingham MK18 1XW. Tel: (0280) 823388